AFTER THE GUNS FALL SILENT

PEACE OR ARMAGEDDON IN THE MIDDLE-EAST

Mohamed Sid-Ahmed
FOREWORD BY LORD CARADON

Translated by MAISSA TALAAT

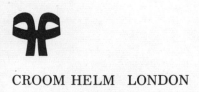

CROOM HELM   LONDON

First published 1976
© 1976 Mohamed Sid-Ahmed

Foreword © 1976 Lord Caradon

Croom Helm Ltd, 2-10 St John's Road, London SW11

ISBN 0-85664-184-7

The English text is a slightly abridged version of the
original Arabic. None of the original argument has been
omitted, but the style and presentation have been adapted
to the western reader.

Printed in Great Britain by Biddles Ltd, Guildford, Surrey

Contents

Lord Caradon's Foreword

A foreword can do three things. It can praise the writer of the book, it can express some reservation on substance, it can put forward a contrary contention.

I am brave enough to attempt all three.

Mohamed Sid-Ahmed is a very experienced journalist, a brilliantly articulate commentator, original, stimulating, constructive. No one can read this book without realising that we have the privilege of listening to a man who thinks clearly and boldly for himself, and who is not afraid to advocate his own unusual and sometimes unpopular conclusions. Here is some fresh thinking and some intricate argument and some honest judgment.

But I have my own reservations. His proposition that some accommodation can be found to avoid another utterly disastrous Middle East war without abandoning extreme positions is ingeniously argued but, I fear, unconvincing.

I do not believe that a settlement can be reached which would satisfy and pacify both Arab rejectionists and Israeli expansionists.

My own view is that there must be an international agreement on the basis of the recognition of both the Israeli homeland and a Palestinian homeland side by side, with sister cities in Jerusalem and no barrier between them. Once this were accepted relationships between the two over open frontiers could start to improve and to move rapidly, I would hope, towards the state of affairs described by Abba Eban some time ago when he said:

> The ultimate guarantee in a peace agreement lies in the creation of common regional interests in such degrees of intensity, in such multiplicity of interaction, in such entanglement of reciprocal advantage, in such accessibility of human contact, as to put the possibility of future war beyond rational contingency.

But such a dream can come true, so I contend, only if both sides start from a position of secure confidence. The key to the new open door to peace must be the recognition of both Israel and a new Palestinian State by the world, and each by the other.

Mohamed Sid-Ahmed shows us in his book the main developments since Resolution 242 was unanimously adopted by the Security Council in November 1967. He well describes the mounting dangers, the growing self-assurance of the Arabs following the 1973 war and, most important of all, the predominant emergence of the cause of the Palestinians, now further reinforced by the local elections on the West Bank. Not even the horrors of the Lebanese conflicts have diminished the importance of that main factor.

So now everything depends, it seems increasingly clear, on rapid advances towards the establishment of a Palestinian homeland in the West Bank and Gaza where the Palestinians can put their talents to work in constructive confidence. My belief is that this can be attained only by a reaffirmation of the principles accepted by all concerned in 1967, and in particular 'the inadmissibility of the acquisition of territory by war' and the right of every State in the area 'to live in peace within secure and recognised boundaries free from threats or acts of force'.

So what is the essence of the disagreement? I believe that in order to avoid another war of devastating proportions it is essential for both sides to start with mutual recognition and move from that to a lasting peace.

We share the same purpose, but Mohamed Sid-Ahmed believes that there is another easier route to escape from the present ominous deadlock.

Read what he says, and see if the persuasive eloquence of his argument can convince you.

June, 1976   Hugh Caradon

Author's Foreword

Two major events have marked the Middle East since this book first appeared in Arabic last year: the second Sinai disengagement agreement and the civil war in Lebanon. Though the two events might appear unrelated, there is a definite connection between them. To the extent that tension between Egypt and Israel was eased beyond the threshold of other Arabs' tolerance, tension in Lebanon rose beyond breaking-point. Arab solidarity, which had been fused by the October war, was shattered. The strife in Lebanon was one expression of this, with implications going much further than the street fighting in Beirut. Traditionally an arena where Arab contrasts and contradictions are played out, Lebanon has been a thermometer of the Arab world and breakdown there is symptomatic of a breakdown on a much wider scale.

Arab thinking has always been inclined to see the Arab-Israeli conflict in absolute terms and any departure from the basic enmity to Israel as abhorrent. The conflict was considered immune to external influences. But this is only true in so far as the basic objectives of the protagonists are irreconcilable. The actual course of the conflict has always proved much more sensitive to the changing international environment.

The Arabs have always regarded their conflict with Israel as one feature of the Arab liberation struggle against western imperialism. The course of this struggle has passed through many stages, all of which were bound to leave their mark on the conflict with Israel. An obvious example of this interplay between the Arab-Israeli *conflict* and the Arab liberation movement's *struggle* against imperialism is the second military round with Israel in 1956. War was declared on Egypt because it nationalised the Suez Canal. Asserting its sovereignty over this vital national asset was a decisive blow to imperialism. Nasser succeeded where Mossadegh had failed. This act of sovereignty ushered in the era of *political independence* for

7

most African countries. Another example of this interplay is the way the fourth military round with Israel in 1973 led the Arabs to use the oil weapon, creating a critical precedent in the Third World's struggle for *economic independence:* OPEC succeeded in raising the price of oil where Allende had failed with copper. The primary producers now had a basis of indexing the price of their exports to the price of finished products in the developed western world.

Not only has the Arab-Israeli conflict been shaped by the underlying confrontation with imperialism (and vice versa), it has also often acted as a catalyst in generating world confrontations. Through this process, far from remaining immune to change, it became more and more acute until, after 1967, it was an endemic crisis and earned the name the Middle East crisis.

It is tempting to regard the October war as a way out of this escalating spiral. It seemed in many ways to put the whole process into reverse and so provide an opportunity for a breakthrough towards a settlement. One central theme of this book will be to examine the impact of the October war and the impact which the international environment has had on the crisis since the onset of détente.

While the 1973 war did remove many of the obstacles in the way of a settlement, it did not generate enough momentum to create the settlement. What it did was to shatter irreversibly the previous pattern of the conflict. But this by no means implies that the only alternative is a settlement. In fact, short of a total breakthrough, the Middle East crisis could become more explosive than ever. The civil war in Lebanon, like the civil war in Spain before World War Two, could be the testing ground for another world conflagration — this time of nuclear dimensions. In such an eventuality, the second Sinai disengagement agreement could well be a second Munich. In other words, unless a settlement comprises all the conflicting parties, including the Palestinians, the conflict could well become even more volcanic. As it is, three trends are bound to acquire increasing importance:

(1) There are grounds for believing that future clashes in the Arab-Israeli conflict could include a nuclear component. In October 1973, for the first time Israel lost its absolute military superiority in terms of conventional weaponry. Now it will

resist having its security entirely dependent on a third party, even the United States. Nor will it be satisfied with international guarantees unless they are backed by an absolute military deterrent. Israel has been trying to go nuclear for years. The measure of its success is unknown, but one thing is certain: if it does have the bomb, the fact that it has been held in reserve in the past is no guarantee for the future. And certainly the growing importance of the Palestinian issue, which threatens the very integrity of the Israeli state, is an additional incentive for the bomb to figure more and more prominently in Israel's calculations.

If Israel brandishes the nuclear threat the Arabs will have no choice but to acquire their own nuclear arsenal. This would further accelerate the proliferation of nuclear weapons which are no longer confined to the great powers. With China and even India now manufacturing their own bomb, there is nothing to prevent the Arabs from following suit. They lack neither the money nor the ability to purchase the necessary technology and to make it work. And if nuclear diplomacy on the global level created détente, it will not necessarily produce the same result in a regional conflict.

(2) The Palestinian issue is expected to become an even more dangerous factor. People have claimed that the Palestinian problem came to prominence in the aftermath of the 1967 débâcle because it was the only inspiration of Arab resistance — a status that it should have lost after the accomplishments of Egypt and Syria in the October war. However, events disproved these expectations: it was after the October war and not before that Arafat was invited to address the UN General Assembly. The recent UN resolution equating Zionism with racism is another significant indication of the Palestinians' growing international stature.

At the same time, the Palestinians within the Arab world have been subjected to ever-increasing harassment. A case in point is the strife in Lebanon. How does one explain the growing impact of the Palestinian issue in the international arena in spite of periodic crackdowns on the Palestinians in the Arab world?[1] One answer is that the Palestinian issue is acquiring new dimensions which go beyond its original character as the core of the Arab-Israeli dispute. It has come to symbolise the coming confrontation between rich and poor countries. The Palestinians' struggle is now an inspiration for the revolt of the dispossessed against the affluent, not only in its ends, but also in its means.

In the developed western world, clear-cut class distinctions allow for the emergence of mass political parties, including left-wing parties, capable of channelling the aspirations of the working classes into revolutionary mass action. Class distinctions are not as clear-cut in underdeveloped societies, where, more often than not, a one-party system covers the whole political gamut. Here dissent and revolt can assume various forms of non-institutionalised violence. Even in developed societies, the institutionalisation of revolutionary parties by the onset of détente has made for the proliferation of a wide spectrum of anti-establishment splinter groups. Indeed, one can now talk of the emergence of a Sixth International, beyond the Comintern (the Third International), the Trotskyites (the Fourth International) and the Maoists (the 'Fifth International'). From guerrilla warfare in the countryside initiated by the Chinese revolution to urban guerrilla warfare developed by the Topamaros, there is a clear continuum now acquiring world proportions. For this Sixth International, the Palestinian resistance is a banner. Stretching from the IRA to the West German Baader-Meinhoff, to the Japanese Red Army, to the Basque militants, it has modelled its techniques along the lines of the Palestinian rejectionist front. The Vienna kidnapping of the OPEC ministers is significant in that the target was neither Israel nor international airlines, but the Arab rich themselves.

(3) The oil weapon has brought extraordinary wealth to the Arab oil-producing countries. However, recycling petrodollars does more for the ills of western welfare economies than it does to serve the development of the Arab peoples. Now with OPEC invited to participate in the dialogue between rich and poor countries, this wealth will also be used as a shield to divert the wrath of the poor countries from the West and it is the Arabs who will be made to pay for the growing gap. Yet another aspect of forthcoming world confrontations being hinged upon the Middle East.

Sandwiched between the nuclear threat (the 'intolerable from above') and the proliferation of terrorism (the 'intolerable from below'), the Arab-Israeli conflict is becoming, more than ever.

the focal point of world confrontations. All these gloomy expectations make a settlement still more imperative. But no stable settlement is conceivable without a clear vision of its mechanics, scope and limitations. This book is an attempt to set out some of the ground rules.

It is an attempt to set forth the unfolding of contradictions in the Middle East crisis as they appear today and as they are most likely to evolve. It is not based on preconceived assumptions. Nor is it an attempt to frame the coming events into an historical determinism, however inevitable we believe this to be. Our object is neither to assume that the region is ultimately bound to follow a socialist path or that it will witness a revival of capitalism. The book concentrates on the most prominent challenges and contradictions which will confront the region in the coming period, a period in which the struggle between capitalism and socialism is acquiring new traits the world over, where the capitalist system is being exposed to deeper crises but where imperialism as a world phenomenon is far from disappearing.

What can be foreseen is the general course of events, their content but not their form, nor the dates at which they will occur. This book is not a polemic on behalf of any one point of view. Rather it tries to sketch likely scenarios for the coming struggle between the conflicting forces operating in the region. Furthermore it does not claim that the prognosis it puts forward will definitely materialise. All it aspires to do is focus attention on a set of likely developments which should not be dismissed in decision-making today.

NOTE

1. Incidentally, it should be noted that whenever the US actively intervene in the peace-making process, the Palestinians are always being harried. When Egypt accepted the Rogers initiative shortly before Nasser's death, the Palestinians were exposed to the Black September massacre in Jordan. When Sadat signed the second Sinai disengagement agreement, once again masterminded by American diplomacy, the Palestinians were under seige in the Lebanon.

PART I: THE OCTOBER WAR — A TURNING-POINT?

1. Whose Victory?

In the year 2000, now only a quarter of a century away, the same distance in time which now separates us from World War Two, history will probably take a very different view of the October war from the Arab and Israeli positions which now prevail. But is it possible with any accuracy to prophesy what the balanced opinion of history will be of these events when passions have cooled? We still live with the consequences of the war all around us and this colours our perceptions, but one fact is certain: twenty-five years hence, the history of the October war will bear little resemblance to the propagandist versions promoted today.

No one will then claim it as a conclusive Arab victory in the terms in which Ahmed Hussein,[1] a self-proclaimed 'chronicler of the nations, and of Egypt in particular', wrote in *Al-Ahram* on 24 October 1973, 'the military victory of Egypt will figure in the most glorious pages in the annals of war and in the history of the Egyptian people.' Future historians will be incredulous at Ahmed Hussein's claim that the October war was a 'divine intervention, a miracle performed by the humble servant of the all-powerful God, Mohamed Anwar el Sadat'. But to envelop the events of October in heroic myth, raising Sadat to the status of a demi-god, is to obscure the true importance of the war.

From the Arab point of view, the October war *was* a 'turning point', a unique event in the history of the nation: crossing the Canal and capturing the Bar-Lev line was regarded as a miracle. Although the occupied territories had not been recaptured and much of the business of the war was still unfinished, national pride was restored and in these terms, the immediate post-war fervour of 'victory' was justified. It produced a feeling that the struggle could now be taken up again with renewed vigour and that the 1967 defeat could be dismissed as an accident and an anomaly. By taking a long-term view of Egyptian history, the Arab press felt able to present the October victory as a natural achievement of Egyptian military history. However, to portray the 'Crossing' as having been a 'crossing from defeat to victory, division to unity, shame to dignity, inequity to justice and from terror to security', as Mustapha Amin[2] wrote on the day he left prison and returned to the political scene, would be a gross oversimplification which no impartial observer could accept.

The war was not a decisive Arab victory any more than it was another decisive Israeli victory (despite several wild assertions to that effect in the days after the war). The Egyptian propaganda was countered by an Israeli version which belittled the crossing of the Canal and the capture of the Bar-Lev line and pointed to Israel's successes on the West Bank of the Canal and on the Golan Heights against Syria. They claimed that but for the intervention of Kissinger, Israeli troops would have maintained their advance towards Suez and destroyed the Egyptian missile bases as well as encircling the Second and Third Armies in Sinai and eliminating all the gains made by Egypt in the first days of the war. But this version was completely untenable even for the Israelis themselves. How else can one explain the campaign of accusation and vilification levelled at the previously highly esteemed leadership? Even Dayan was now called a 'liar' and a 'demagogue'; they were all branded 'assassins', jointly responsible for the casualties which far exceeded the experience of earlier wars. What else could explain the collapse of the Meir government at the first elections after the war, her withdrawal from public life, the departure of Eban and Dayan from power, and the eclipse of many other figures who had long been the living symbols of the 'invincible and infallible state of Israel'?

On 8 October, two days after the war began, Dayan declared during his press conference, 'We have no political objectives in this war. We want to inflict a defeat, rob them of any gains they may make and force them to pay for what they have done.' This confident tone was echoed by other Israeli voices. That same day, Zeev Shiff, who was close to the High Command, closed his article in *Haaretz* with, 'We must cross the Canal and establish our forces on the West Bank, not to occupy more territory but to make sure that the Egyptians will have no temptation in the near future, neither on the day of Yom Kippur nor on any other day, to resort to arms.' On the following day another commentator, Dan Shiftan, said that this war must leave 'painful scars for the Arabs like the loss of territories in June 1967.' He went on to say:

> One way to achieve such an end is to move in the direction of systematic destruction of the economic base, the means of communication and natural resources. In Egypt, for instance, it is possible to hit the large industrial complex in Helwan and set fire to the oil fields. In Syria we must try in addition to expand the occupied stretch and pose a permanent threat to Damascus from our artillery.

In these proposals Israel's objectives were clearly revealed: (1) to make the Arabs pay dearly for having dared to defy them; (2) to teach them a lesson which would dissuade them from ever trying it again; (3) to preserve the equilibrium which they had established by the conquests of 1967.

For the Israelis, the Canal represented a secure frontier, a position of strength to be abandoned only for other secure frontiers to be negotiated with Egypt on Israel's terms.[3] In launching the October war Sadat upset their calculations and Israel reacted with rage. However, none of its avowed objectives were achieved. If Egypt and Syria in waging the war were prepared to make sacrifices, Israel actually suffered much greater sacrifices in terms of relative human and material resources. Instead of being taught a lesson, the Arab armies were rehabilitated in combat and recovered their honour. This was an irreversible phenomenon. On the other hand, the Israeli army turned out to be neither as powerful nor as invulnerable as its generals had claimed. By laying bare deficiencies so serious that they could not be dismissed, its image of invincibility was cracked. This was an intolerable phenomenon. The pre-October 1973 equilibrium was definitely upset. As a result of the disengagement agreements on both fronts, Israel has already withdrawn not only from the West, but also from the East Bank of the Canal and has abandoned Kuneitra on the Golan Heights. To talk of a victory more startling than that of 1967, when Israel had failed so manifestly to achieve any of the objectives it set itself, is sheer nonsense.

But if there was no decisive victory for the Arabs nor for the Israelis, what was the outcome of the October war? Had it, as Mohammed Heikal* suggested on 9 November 1973, changed

*Then Editor of *Al-Ahram.*

the situation of 'no-war, no-peace' into one of 'no-victory, no-defeat'? Had the state of 'immobility', in Heikal's phrase, been transformed into a new phase of 'movement'? We can understand the true effects of October 1973 only when we appreciate what benefits each protagonist derived from the war and which profited most from the outcome.

In the Arab-Israeli conflict, the terms 'victory' and 'defeat' have a particular meaning which is quite different from their accepted usage. Under the rules of this game, unless Israel produces a victory that no one can challenge, it loses; and as soon as the Arabs avoid a 'crushing defeat', they can claim a victory of significance. This anomaly is due to the particular conditions of the conflict, which, reduced to a simple formula, match Israeli 'quality' against Arab 'quantity'. By Israeli 'quality', we mean the infrastructure and institutions of an advanced society, its human potential and military superiority, however limited its territory, population and material resources. By Arab 'quantity' we mean an abundance of territory, population and natural resources without the structure of a developed society.

These two conditions, so fundamentally different, could remain in perpetual antagonism without the introduction of a common measure: neither side would ever be able to exhaust the other. For, however brilliant their victories, the Israelis can never subdue the vast extent of the Arab world. Indeed, any territorial extension of the state of Israel, any neo-Roman Empire built out of Arab lands, would only dilute the concept of a Zionist state, 'a national home for the Jewish people'. On the other hand, Arab 'quantity', forming part of the Third World, has no hope at this juncture of overpowering Israeli 'quality'.

Now if the October war does mark a new stage in the history of the conflict it is because it introduced a notion of parity, 'commensurability', between the parties. For the first time the Arabs proved that they had the measure of Israeli 'quality' on the battlefield; so too certain features of Arab 'quantity', like petroleum, gave them a qualitative edge, even if it was the energy crisis which provided a totally extraneous reason. Conversely, Israel no longer has the capacity to compensate for this disadvantage with some 'qualitative' endeavour; it could threaten to resort to the ultimate weapon, the nuclear bomb, but to do this would be akin to Samson destroying the Temple and burying himself in the ruins. In addition, the source of Israel's 'quantitative' growth is drying up: Jewish immigration has slowed down since Israel lost its previous stability. In this new situation a fresh equation is being constructed which contains a common denominator in the parity between the parties. In this new equation the notation means the same thing to both parties and this is a change which cannot be underestimated when we analyse the future of the conflict.

NOTES

1. In 1936, at the time of the Anglo-Egyptian Treaty, he founded a Fascist-style party called Young Egypt (Misr el Fatah). In the absence of any socialist or internationalist element in Egyptian politics, this party reflected the attraction that Nazi Germany had for a section of the nationalist petit bourgeois who were opposed to all the existing parties' compromise with Great Britain and that included the main nationalist party, the Wafd. On the eve of the revolution in 1952, Ahmed Hussein turned his party, now styled the Socialist Party, to violent diatribes against the palace and the feudal landowners and was accused of having participated in the burning of Cairo on 26 January 1952.
2. Together with his twin brother Ali Amin he founded the newspaper *Akhbar-El-Yom* immediately after World War Two. Although very close to the palace and the Americans, the Amin brothers survived the events of 1952 and realigned themselves with Nasser, collaborating for a long time with the new regime. In 1965 Mustapha Amin was accused of spying for the CIA and sentenced to life imprisonment. He was released at the beginning of 1974 and returned to *Akhbar-el-Yom* as editor.
3. It was the Israelis themselves who chose not to cross the Canal immediately after the Six Day war because they regarded it as an impregnable barrier against the Egyptians. After the occupation of Sinai it provided a 'natural and ideal frontier' for a secure Israel. To have gone any further would have done them more harm than good, because it would have meant occupying the fertile land of the fellah instead of desert, in a region which for more than a hundred years had been at the heart of Egyptian modernisation, and a focal point in the development of the nationalist movement.

2. The Search for 'a Common Measure'

What are we to make of this element of parity, commensurability, this common denominator, indeed, this language whose terminology can perhaps be equally understood by all the parties to the conflict? Firstly we must be more precise; obviously there can be no question of a common political ideology, or psychological or ethnic affinity after twenty-five years of intense hostility and total antagonism. This is especially true in so far as the Arab-Israeli conflict does not fit the generally accepted classification of the major conflicts the world has known since World War Two. It is peculiar in that it has been almost impervious to the changes in the international climate brought about by the move from Cold War to détente. At least until the October war the conflict was distinguished by clear polarisation, characteristic of the Cold War.

The Arabs can indeed be accused of excesses — in reality more verbal than actual — in the formulation of their aims. However, their grievance can hardly be called in question, for it is in the category of the legitimate claims of national liberation movements; the restitution of territory occupied by force and the right of the Palestinian people to self-determination — claims recognised in the Charter and confirmed by the resolutions of the United Nations. On the other hand, there is no unanimous world opinion on the 'fact of Israel': how far is it a special case which is not simply 'colonialism' or 'racism'; on what grounds can its survival be justified?

In fact, in so far as the setting up of Israel as a settler state, further aggravated by a systematic policy of annexation, did inflict injustice on the Arabs, many international parties involved in the crisis do not conclude that the removal of this injustice requires the suppression of Israel. Nor do they feel that the restitution of the Arabs' legitimate rights need presuppose the denial of other 'rights', also 'legitimate', which came into being with the creation of Israel. These parties argue

20

that this should not be obscured by Israel's own behaviour, whether racist or expansionist, or indeed by Israel's placing itself in the imperialist orbit to protect itself against Arab rejection. This opinion is not simply the view of 'imperialist circles', but is also held by a considerable portion of world opinion, including the socialist countries that continually voice their full support for the Arab cause.

Israeli society has fundamental inconsistencies that the Arabs have not been alone in perceiving:

(1) The Zionist project is to have a homeless people ('the chosen race') return to a people-less country ('the promised land'): but to accommodate less than a fifth of world Jewry in Palestine, two-thirds of the native population have had to be expelled;

(2) The invocation of religious, mythical, anachronistic reasoning to justify the existence of Israel, and the inability to sustain that existence by other than ultra-modern methods, which are scientific, areligious and non-mythical *par excellence;*

(3) Israel comprises the Ashkenazy of Germany, Poland, America, the Sephardi of Spain, the Balkans and North Africa, the eastern Jews of Arab origin, the Jews of India and Ethiopia. If persecution can be invoked as a reason for them to leave their places of origin, the myth of a common origin going back several thousand years is not sufficient to give them a coherent and stable identity without it being artificially fostered by the hostility of their environment.

(4) Since its foundation it has survived only through foreign assistance which on a *per capita* basis has been five times larger than the aid given to any other country in the world, including South Vietnam, South Korea and Formosa.[1]

(5) Israel insists that the security of a state can be guaranteed, while at the same time refusing any attempt to define its own borders;

(6) The Zionist wish to preserve the Jewish character of Israel, at the same time refusing to abandon an annexationist policy. Indeed, according to one calculation, there will be in a single generation more people of Arab origin, Jewish or non-Jewish, within the borders at present occupied by Israel, simply by demographic pressure, which favours the eastern Jews at the expense of the western ones, and the non-Jewish Arabs at the expense of the Jews.

These contradictions deprive Israel of the elements of cohesion needed for the stability of any state, but they do not deprive Israel, in the eyes of a considerable portion of world opinion, of its right to exist. Even if we do not accord validity to the very idea of a 'Jewish state', whatever the persecutions suffered by the Jews through the centuries and culminating in Nazism; even if we deliberately ignore the injustice of making a third party, the Arabs, suffer the consequences of these persecutions, there will always be those who say that it was the systematic resistance put up by the Arabs to the Jewish state that crystallised an Israeli identity, an 'Israeli nation'. In the same way, the systematic aversion shown by the Jewish state towards the Palestinians may be said to have crystallised a Palestinian identity, a Palestinian nation. In history, we can never turn the clock back. We have to take account of acquired 'rights', particularly when considering the future.

If the 'right' is absolute, both for the Israelis and Palestinians, there can be question only of partitioning the land of Palestine and not the 'right' itself between those who claim it on their side. Many people of such opinion deny neither the Arab nor the Palestinian right; their opinion is very different from the Arabs', but many of them have a sincere wish to arrive at an equitable settlement infringing the rights of neither side. It is with such arguments in mind that they seek commensurability, a common language that can serve as a basis for a settlement.

The relevance of such an approach to the problem lies in the fact that in historical perspective it will be regarded as having lacked bias, subjectivity, emotional commitment or incidental interference. In presenting their case, the parties to the conflict cannot avoid adapting their arguments to the logic of this approach. Moreover, the elements of the conflict are of such complexity that it is almost futile to try and convince third parties that 'right' is on one side alone and 'wrong' entirely on the other. Thus the search for common ground in the conflict forces us to transcend ideological, political, social or other criteria readily applicable in other cases.

Shock Therapy

On 23 April 1973, almost six months before the October war, Arnaud de Borchgrave wrote in *Newsweek:*

Though they would never admit it publicly, Washington's policy-makers no longer dismiss Sadat's repeated vows to change the political equation in the Middle East by means of a political 'shock'. Even more startling, these top-level Americans privately concede that (1) there is little the US can do to head off a resumption of hostilities in the Middle East and (2) such an explosion might even have a 'salutary impact'. 'It is a sad fact of Middle Eastern life today', commented one of these officials, 'that a political settlement does not seem possible without a major crisis first'.

He goes on to conclude:

One interesting footnote to the present diplomatic breakdown in the Middle East is that many Arab leaders have asked me whether Henry Kissinger will soon take over the American search for a Middle East peace settlement. After a week in Washington, I doubt it seriously. Vietnam is still not wrapped up neatly, and there is also the whole complex bag of European affairs to concern Mr. Nixon's chief foreign-policy adviser. Moreover, Kissinger is not a man to undertake a diplomatic mission that does not have a reasonable chance of success. In the current Middle East situation, there is no such chance. Cairo insists that it will not concede an inch of Arab land to the Israelis. And the Israelis are satisfied with the present status quo — as are many Americans. The next move is Sadat's. Afterwards perhaps it will be time for Dr. Kissinger's considerable diplomatic skills to be called into play.

Just a few days after this article appeared, De Borchgrave told me during a conversation in *Al-Ahram* that the prominent personality he had talked of was Kissinger himself, and that he had said, 'I never handle crises cold; to solve them, they have to be "hot" for me to see what should be accorded to each of the parties. We cannot consider what the parties were six years before. . .or two thousand years ago!'[2]

Should we then conclude that the Arab decision to wage war on 6 October suited American purpose; that it was simply an 'experimental' war resulting from a convergence of design intended to bring an end to the passive situation of 'no-war, no-peace' and actively generate peace through war? Was the war merely the trigger, the salutary shock, required to promote the common denominator indispensable to a political settlement of the crisis?

But with the casualties on both sides the October war showed itself to be a bloody collision, ample evidence of a very real antagonism which could not be reduced to an 'experimental' war. Never before had combat between Arabs and Israelis been waged with such ferocity, and for once the Egyptian blood shed in the Sinai has not been in vain. In improving Arab prestige, it raised the self-esteem of the Arab and the Arab soldier. Thus Arab solidarity, which had come to take on a pejorative meaning, returned to life and, as if by magic, was turned into a concerted effort: with their blood spilt on the battlefield, the Arabs cut off their oil. The Arab world had, overnight, acquired a new presence. The blood shed in combat testified to the eruption from below of a popular mass force which foiled any political manipulation from above. It was the emergence of this force that was to give the war its liberating character. But the most remarkable feat of the war was that a vital myth was shattered — the myth of the Israeli David against the Arab Goliath, the Israeli superman of supernatural quality facing a race of congenitally backward inferiors: an argument put above and widely spread in Israeli sociological analyses following the Six Day war.

After Egyptian air strength had been wiped out in 1956 as in 1967 on the ground, the land army of Sinai lost air cover; for the Egyptian soldier, harassed by the desert sun, the massacre inflicted on him by successive waves of supersonic aircraft was a bloody apocalypse. In the October war electronics was no longer the intangible angel of death: it was a man-to-man war, motorised but equal. It was primarily on this level that a new basis for a 'common measure' was created.

What is new since the October war is a set of circumstances which have fostered an awareness on both the Israeli and Arab sides that a *modus vivendi* in some mutually acceptable peace settlement would be the lesser evil. For Israel there now exists cause to buttress the argument that a condition for its survival in the medium to long term is to admit that the Arab environment, indeed even the Palestinians, may no longer be dismissed. The Zionist thesis that the return to the promised land is the return of a homeless people to a land empty of people can no longer be adopted by Israel. On the other hand, an increasing Arab persuasion feels more and more that the ever greater 'cost' of the war and its ever more demanding requirements may be too much at the expense of the proper mobilisation of their human and material resources for development.

To set as an aim a 'just peace' is thus a credible objective now possible for the first time since the October war. This does not mean that this objective will actually be attained, or that it is the only possibility for the future. But that possibility, hitherto not even on the cards, is now an option. The possibility of peace was not there before the October war because the Arabs had not previously felt any sense of a common measure with the enemy, although Israeli 'quality', whatever its superiority, had never been able to exhaust or finish off Arab 'quantity'. However, even today there is no unanimity in the admission that some settlement of the conflict has now become necessary or even desirable. The rejectionist front, the dissident movement emerging from the Palestinian resistance, illustrates the fact that in the Arab world there are still many who persist in rejecting adamantly any solution. However, it can be demonstrated with almost mathematical rigour that Arab stigmatisations of Israel have been extreme in language in direct proportion to their frustration at the inadequacy of action. In the Arab world, non-commensurability with the enemy has been reflected in an equally striking non-commensurability between words and deeds, proclaiming goals and actual accomplishments.

Yasser Arafat has been able to set as his goal the creation of a democratic secular state in Palestine, open to Jewish, Christian and Moslem populations alike. This is an undeniable advance from the earlier slogan attributed to Shukeiry of 'throwing the Jews into the sea'. What concerns us here is not whether Arafat's objective is actually attainable in the short or medium term, but that after achieving tangible results since July 1967 (notably the famous battle of Karame) at the nadir of Arab despair, Al Fatah was able, unlike the PLO before June 1967, to put forward more credible objectives.

If Nasser was the first Arab leader to accept Resolution 242 of the Security Council, which implied acceptance of the fact of

Israel's existence, it was because despite the defeats of 1967, he, more than any other Arab leader, could claim credit for fifteen years of revolution.

But it could also be demonstrated with no less mathematical rigour that there has always been a 'correspondence' between the Arab confrontation with Israel and internal developments within the Arab world over the last quarter of a century. It was the utter failure of the Arabs to prevent the establishment of the Israeli state of 15 May 1948 that was behind the Revolution in Egypt of 23 July 1952. Indeed the fire of revolution ignited in Egypt gradually stretched to many Arab countries. 'Correspondence' does not imply 'commensurability'. Not being able to expunge the shame of the 1948 defeat and act effectively against the Israeli usurpation, the Egypt of the 1952 Revolution responded by focusing its attention on rebuilding its internal structure, which was to gradually acquire a revolutionary, anti-colonial and anti-imperialist character. This did not require immediate 'commensurability' with the initial enemy, but it did provide a much needed and legitimate source of national pride and social progress without having recourse to a trial of arms with Israel with its unforeseen consequences.

The failure of the tripartite attack in 1956 was also hardly conclusive as regards achievement of a 'common measure' between Israel and Egypt. Indeed precisely on this point it could on the contrary be misleading: thanks to Soviet and American intervention, the failure was political, not military. The Soviets sought to defend the anti-colonial achievements of Egypt and the Arab world and the Americans wanted to substitute American influence in the vacuum left by the defeat of the British and the French by means of the Eisenhower Doctrine. If 1956 had magnified out of all proportion the Arab self-image *vis-à-vis* Israel, June 1967 did much the same thing *vis-à-vis* the Arabs. Both phenomena acted against the achievement of any 'common measure'.

After 1967, the apparent inability of the Arabs to demonstrate their parity with the enemy had various consequences: they lost credibility in the outside world; they expressed distrust for the United States and proclaimed friendship for the USSR, in both cases more voiced than felt; inter-Arab relations were often vitiated by extreme vacillations from attempts at 'total unity' to violent and pointless animosity.

The Balance of Power

It is relevant to recall here that the balance of power between belligerents in any conflict is always the outcome of a whole set of factors: economic, social, political, ideological and military. One of the characteristics of *blitzkrieg* modern warfare is the disproportionate importance that the military element may have at the expense of the others, particularly if one of the belligerents is much better equipped to handle ultra-modern weaponry. In the light of this, people were inclined to regard the Arab potential after 1967 as having being reduced in proportion to the scale of their military defeat and to regard Israel's potential as commensurate with its military victory, without taking other factors into account. Both impressions were wrong but they had to be proved. It was this that made the October war inevitable, because any purely political solution without military intervention would have been unable to overcome the impasse of the no-peace, no-war situation. After 1967 people were too inclined to see in the Arab world only the centrifugal forces of disintegration and decomposition. They did not notice that these centrifugal forces could also induce a reverse process, stimulating a vigorous self-criticism, a profound re-examination of the reasons for such a crushing defeat. On the other hand, Israel tended to rest on its laurels in a euphoric view of its own power, unhesitatingly displaying greater and greater arrogance. But Israel is strong only in proportion to its appearance of weakness; it loses its strength once its claimed 'weakness' is no longer credible. This paradox became plain in June 1967 although Israel did not have to pay the price until October 1973.

When the Arabs unleashed their offensive of 6 October, there were theoretically three objectives which could be imputed to them: to exterminate the state of Israel, as the intention had been attributed to the Arabs on the eve of June 1967; to liberate the Arab territories occupied by Israel after June 1967, a right that cannot be contested; and to defy the myth of the invincibility of the Israeli doctrine of security, based on occupation of Arab land, force Israel to renounce its obstinacy in not returning these lands, to end the impasse of no-war, no-peace and to open, through war, the way to peace, without war being the only means of achieving such a goal.

The third of these objectives, which does not even

incorporate the legitimate liberation of all their lands by military means, was clearly at the base of the Egyptian-Syrian strategy. In reality this strategy did not simply comprise a military phase, or even both military and political phases. It was conceived to include three phases: a military one, enough to provoke a phase of concerted Arab intervention, introducing the oil weapon, thus producing the conditions for the third political phase capable of bringing a solution to the crisis. It was through this three-pronged strategy that the Arabs sought to achieve parity as a condition for a breakthrough towards a just settlement.

In any event, Israel was to persist in not recognising this parity, this 'common denominator'. War, for Israel, was a 'shock', but in a sense quite different from that foreseen by Arnaud de Borchgrave. 'Shock' for him meant a 'laboratory war' which, though it would probably have disastrous consequences for the Arabs, could end the impasse. Things turned out quite differently. In reality, what took place was a 'real war', the intensity of which was unrivalled in the region and it was Israel which had to face the consequences.

In the days following the war Israeli commentators were furiously denying that the previous set-up had been irreversibly destroyed. They also refused to accept that a new balance of power, introducing a new element of parity, had been achieved. To appreciate this, it is sufficient to read the Israeli press of that period. On 2 November 1973 General Ezer Weizman wrote in *Maariv:* 'The successes of the Egyptians and Syrians, in the first days of the war, were not the result of an improvement of their ability, but of errors on our part.' The implication is that the Arabs are by definition inferior, unable to improve their military performance; the Israelis are by definition superior. If they were defeated, and if their enemies were victorious, then it was because of accidents, 'negligence' and 'mistakes'. This was also *Likoud's* interpretation of the 'negligence' that the Agranat Commission was to examine. *Likoud* put it down to 'tactical errors, regrettable failures which can be rectified without our slipping into a policy of abandonment and defeatism'. The same implication came up in press commentaries that would ascribe Arab successes only to Soviet assistance, and picture them as the outcome of 'Soviet planning, Soviet training and Soviet equipment'. What would they have said if the Soviet military experts had still been in Egypt at the beginning of hostilities? Harkaby uses the same logic: 'One of the chief reasons for our losing our sense of perspective is the inbalance between our military strength and our political power.' The implication in this is that the politicians betrayed the generals. In effect, this could read: 'We could have inflicted a crushing defeat on the Egyptian forces. We were forced by the cease-fire to stop.' What Harkaby will not appreciate is that the statesmen were better placed to see that they had no choice but to conform to the restraints from which Israel cannot free itself.

These attempts to reduce military failures to the level of 'negligence' which, painful as may have been the useless sacrifice of human life, nonetheless could have been remedied, were still not enough to reassure a public opinion traumatised by the shock, nor did they give satisfactory answers to questions that the war could only put forward: hence the eruption of a dissent movement not prepared to brush aside the relevant questions. In fact when it is admitted that the Israeli intelligence services had not been badly informed as to Egyptian intentions but had rather, despite American warnings, wrongly analysed the information they gathered, clearly there is no technical error involved. It is a much more serious fault of interpretation, showing a defective political judgement of the situation. In fact, the discussions which tore Israeli society apart just after the war were concerned with a great deal more than simple defects in the super-structure. They reflected in Israeli terms much deeper problems involving the very foundations of the Israeli edifice and touched on those basic inconsistencies which the Arabs, as well as impartial observers, had long since spotted even when the edifice seemed unshakeable. It was this sudden awareness of these fundamental truths that provoked a dismal confusion throughout various parts of the Israeli society which assumed earthquake proportions. Whatever the degree to which the country's institutions have been able to absorb this internal explosion, one fact is certain: the October war will leave indelible traces and will have irreversibly marked Israel's way of thinking.

NOTES

1. This aid, if taken *per capita* by Egypt, would have meant a sum three times greater than the whole of American aid to all countries of the world since the end of World War Two.
2. Kissinger meant the period just after the Six Day war, or the moment of Jewish dispersal by the Romans.

3. Israel Between Doves and Hawks

What changes have occurred in the structure of the Israeli edifice since the October war? Potentially if not in fact the Israeli quest for survival has always been subject to two logics which, though apparently contradictory, are in fact complementary.

The first, which focuses on immediate interests regardless of any long-term concern, is the hawks' 'big-stick' policy. In a hostile environment, they reckon that Israel's existence can only be guaranteed by absolute military superiority, invulnerability, and an ability to respond with devastating efficiency to any Arab threat. This argument implies total non-commensurability with the Arabs, if not for blatant racialist reasons, at least under the pretext of incompatible strategic and geopolitical interests.

The second logic is against sacrificing long-term interest for short-term gain. It is the logic of the 'carrot' — the doves. They argue that coexistence with the Arab environment is sooner or later inevitable. To suppose that Israel's interests are fundamentally incompatible with those of its surroundings damages in their view the evolution towards this inevitable coexistence and must provoke Arab reaction likely to threaten still more the very existence of Israel. The doves are not opposed in principle to the idea of 'commensurability' being a basic part of the quest for a *modus vivendi*. This 'common measure' — a 'common language' — would be for them not only the shrewdest way of assuring the survival of Israel, but also the best way to perpetuate its privileged position while defusing the possibility of increasing danger.

Israel has indeed experienced, in the course of its history, various expressions of dissidence on the part of its intelligentsia, various parties and movements that have rejected Zionism more or less consistently. Some of these parties and movements, particularly the Communist Party Rakah, but also Matzpen, the Land Movement and others, have displayed considerable courage in contesting the validity of Zionism in the very interest of world Jewry. They have most vigorously denounced the dangers of the aggressive and expansionist policy of the Israeli leaders, particularly when they were at the height of their conceit following the Six Day war. Nonetheless, these parties remain marginal, much stronger in the Arab minority than in the heart of Israeli society. Their impact has been limited and without effect on official policy. The Israeli establishment tolerates their existence less out of anxiety to preserve the image of 'Israeli democracy' than to use them as antennae in assessing sensitive issues which might deserve its attention.

Before the October war, and particularly after the Six Day war, the situation was obviously in the hawks' favour. A clear sign of this is the Galilee document, officially adopted by the *Maarech* for the Knesset elections held on the eve of the war, a document that codified creeping annexationism. The argument of the annexationists was that to restore the land taken in 1967 would sooner or later lead to the collapse of the state, for the dynamics of territorial expansion must undergo no retreat. The doves argued that this policy must lead to another war but their objections were in vain so long as such a war had not occurred. Their presence in the establishment was tolerated only in so far as it provided a useful window dressing.

The October war had sufficient impact to give the doves a more important function than simple window dressing, though not sufficient to invalidate all the hawks' arguments. The failure of the traditional line, the downfall of its proponents, the spread of a dissident movement, the isolation in which Israel finds itself, the restraints placed upon it by international détente, all this is evidence for the doves' case. It is not by chance that some of the most notorious doves, Arie Eliav or Ben Aharon, resigned in a spectacular way in order to emphasise their disapproval of official policy at a time when such attitudes were certain to influence a wider public. But the hawks could retort that precisely because specific links in the previous security system had been shown defective, it was more vital than ever for the state to make itself less vulnerable, even at the price of a new military round. Israel has thus since the

October war been victim to opposing attitudes. Both seek to ensure its survival, but along diametrically opposed lines of action. This rift threatens to block the difficult decisions that can no longer be put off and imbues them with a certain hesitancy and lack of initiative. This has been all the more true since the eclipse of Israel's traditional stars and the collapse of its leaders who had been above party strife and internal dispute and who alone were able to take painful decisions without being exposed to an avalanche of hostile and paralysing criticism. This is probably the greatest single threat to a settlement. The idea of commensurability with its neighbours remains unacceptable to a considerable proportion of Israeli opinion. However, the Israelis cannot decide alone on this issue, for it has to be stressed that both the superpowers have been anxious to further such commensurability between the belligerents.

Superpower Intervention

Were it only for their furnishing of weaponry, superpower intervention in the conflict would have been unavoidable. Throughout the October war, it has marked the course and outcome of operations, if only through the particular importance of the military element in the conflict and its dependence on the quality and quantity of arms at the belligerents' disposal. This was true not only for the Arabs, for whether it was determined by this factor or not, the 'turning-point' of the war had only come once a massive airlift had supplied Israel with ultra-modern military equipment, shattering the legend of Israel's independence *vis-à-vis* its protector. In fact Soviet and American intervention was both to intensify and limit military operations: intensifying them through the supply of increasingly sophisticated and destructive arms, but also limiting both the duration and range of the war through the rapid consumption of these ultra-costly weapons and the threat that escalation might have for détente.

The Americans and Soviets intervened in the conflict with opposite intentions. For the Soviet Union, it was vital to prove that peaceful coexistence does not imply renunciation of the objectives of national liberation. The Americans, on their side, wished not only to defend Israel and preserve the reputation of their military equipment, but also to defend vital American

interests affected by the oil weapon. Although favourable to
Israel, Kissinger's diplomacy has not sought to prevent the
Arab countries from obtaining military results likely to
encourage them to take initiatives of a bolder kind at the
diplomatic level. He refused to allow Israel to be either
victorious or defeated because it would have made a
breakthrough in the direction of a settlement more difficult to
obtain. However contradictory the motivation of the two
superpowers, such an American strategy did not encounter
outright Soviet opposition.

This intervention changed the whole set-up in the Middle
East and introduced the rules of détente. To understand the
impact of this change, we must first establish what détente
means.

PART II: THE INTERNATIONAL DIMENSION

4. Détente — A New System or Chaos?

Dr Henry Kissinger is said to have made détente possible. A Harvard professor, who had been national security adviser to the President, then latterly his Secretary of State, was credited with having devised a new mode of negotiation which successfully transformed Nixon's avowed objective to replace confrontation with co-operation into a living reality. Nor is it the American mass media alone which sings Kissinger's praises, for he enjoys the esteem of many world leaders, including those most hostile to US policies. Sadat, for example, has repeatedly extolled the Secretary's genius, and described him as a trustworthy intermediary. I remember one private discussion which I had in Moscow in September 1973 with Professor Arbatov, the head of the US Institute in the Soviet Union; he acknowledged the undeniable talents of Kissinger, though he opposed his political philosophy on security and upheld the notion of 'collective security'. But the strangest judgement came from Chou en Lai, when he spoke to the *Al-Ahram* team in February 1973. 'We are against Israel', he remarked, 'but not against the Jews. Many great men in history have been Jewish: Marx, Einstein — and Kissinger.'

But the fact remains that despite the glowing testimonials to Kissinger's genius from friend and foe alike, the shift in American policy from Cold War to détente was dictated by objective factors.[1] One main incentive was the need to retain US leadership of the western world. When the United States had acquired this position after World War Two, Europe and Japan were devastated by the ravages of war. Through the Marshall Plan, the United States pumped new resources into the shattered European economies, and secured the defence of European capitalism, militarily, through NATO. In exchange for this military and economic assistance, Europe had to acknowledge the unchallenged leadership of the US; the same was true for Japan, which had been brought to its knees by Hiroshima and Nagasaki. But changes gradually came about within the western alliance, and the US realised that competition, both economic and political, was beginning to threaten the cohesion of the alliance: brandishing the 'Communist Threat', in the manner of John Foster Dulles, was no longer effective in concealing the growing divergences among the allies. So the Americans devised a new strategy which would ensure the continuation of their leading role.

It was at this point that Kissinger emerged on the scene. His initiatives in dealing with the socialist camp did not stem from the growing rifts in the western alliance alone, for changes in the global balance of power compelled the United States to revise its policy of pushing confrontation to the brink. Science and technology were no longer monopolised by the US and the developed western world. The Soviet Union emerged as a major competitor, scoring many spectacular 'firsts': their triumphs in the space race, and in the development of highly sophisticated weapon systems, were pointed reminders to the West of the power and resilience of the socialist world. For the West, in fact, there was no choice except to reduce tension, and to explore means of limiting the arms race, especially in the field of strategic arms. For the first time, even the most die-hard imperialists were concerned to avoid collective suicide. In the context of this new balance of power and especially since most of the colonies in the Third World had acquired political independence, the sterility of the traditional colonial policy of overt aggression became apparent. The most glaring example of this was Vietnam: not only did the US fail to achieve a decisive military victory, but suffered a political backlash at home as well. The only exception may have been the Middle East because of the specific character of the crisis, and the difficulty of classifying it within the obvious patterns of confrontation between imperialism and national liberation movements.

Thus America was spurred to abandon its policy of Cold War brinkmanship both by deterrents and the incentives of extricating itself from Vietnam and reasserting its leadership over the western alliance. So it began to consider a new policy towards the socialist countries.

The Sino-Soviet dispute came as a godsend to the United States, for it created a yawning chasm in the unity of the socialist community. At no time did the US give up trying to drive a wedge between the USSR and China, not even at the height of the Cold War. In retrospect, the United States" insistence on keeping People's China out of the UN for many years now seems due to more than unswerving support for Nationalist China. Whilst the US had to keep the international forum open to the USSR at all times, it treated People's China as an outcast. This certainly had something to do with the charge of collusion with imperialism which Mao's regime levelled against the Soviet Union.

As soon as American policy-makers were sure that the quarrel between the two socialist giants had reached the point of no return, Kissinger made his first secret trip to Peking. This gave the United States a new gambit in its relations with the Soviet Union and a means of bringing the Vietnam war to an end, relieving the Americans of the unbearable burden of endless Asiatic wars aimed at encircling China. It was an ideal face-saving solution, compensating for the lack of a decisive military victory by a brilliant political manoeuvre. America's allies both favoured and feared this new policy. They welcomed the end of the effective embargo which the US had imposed on exchanges with the socialist world, which was harming the economies of both Europe and Japan, and poisoning the political atmosphere. Yet they feared the *rapprochement* between the great powers, which could threaten their own freedom of manoeuvre.

But Kissinger obviously achieved brilliant results, with Nixon's historic visit to China in February 1972, the first Summit with the Soviet leaders in May 1972, and the Vietnam agreement in January 1973. By then the world was acclaiming the 'Kissinger miracle', and both friends and enemies were loud in their praise. Kissinger was said to have outstripped even Metternich and Bismarck, on whom he had consciously modelled himself: his star rose rapidly and he paved the way to Nixon's sweeping victory in the presidential election of November 1972.

It soon became apparent that the United States' growing relationship with its opponents, specifically the USSR, was provoking suspicions and susceptibilities among its allies. It seemed that Kissinger's negotiations were most successful when he dealt with the opposite camp. Obvious cracks began to appear in NATO. Gaullist France was no longer the only

European country to pursue a more independent policy. Kissinger tried to make 1973 the 'Year of Europe' to mend the rift and restore cohesion. But towards the end of that year the October war broke out. With the use of the oil weapon, the rift deepened. Kissinger's prediction failed, and 1973 was the 'Year of the Middle East' instead of the 'Year of Europe'.

I remember an interesting discussion at the International Institute of Strategic Studies conference in September 1974 on the world impact of the October war. A debate arose between the European participants and their American counterparts. Many Europeans firmly stated their refusal to accept the argument of western solidarity as a justification for forcing Europe into unconditional acceptance of the American point of view. They claimed that Europe had as much right to strive towards building a strategic solidarity with the Arabs in defence of its economic interests and to ensure the flow of oil imported from the Arab countries as it had a duty to preserve its strategic solidarity with the US in defence of the West's political structure.

The American speakers criticised Europe's non-compliance with what they considered vital to the basic western interests. They were astonished that the European countries did not provide the US with landing facilities during its airlift to Israel in the war, forcing American planes to use the longer route via the Azores. The European speakers, in their turn, expressed their discontent. They questioned the right of the US to object to the declaration issued by the EEC on 6 November 1973 in which they set out a more friendly stand towards the Arabs. The also questioned whether the US's unilateral declaration of a nuclear alert on 25 October, exposing Europe to the danger of a total confrontation with the USSR, was justified. No doubt the European leaders are satisfied with the US's policy to curtail Soviet 'influence', but certainly not if it is to be at the expense of vital European interests affecting their oil sources, their balance of payments, their security and their vulnerability to the ills of inflation.

What is true for Europe is true also for Japan. The US's sudden *rapprochement* with China threatened the foundations of Japan's strategy in the Far East and disturbed the stability of the political equation on which its security was built. Japan had no choice but to end its hostile stand towards China. It was in these circumstances that the Arabs used the oil weapon. Japan's economy was deeply shaken when the oil flow was cut down. With a threatened drop in its rate of growth from an average of 10 to 5 per cent, Japan was forced to challenge the US, and adopt a more sympathetic stand towards the Arabs. In this way it hoped to guarantee its oil flow by a more active presence in the Arab world, until it could diversify its sources of energy, probably by obtaining more of its oil from China.

What is the explanation for Kissinger's success in dealing with his government's opponents and his failure in dealing with its allies? Kissinger excels in bilateral negotiations, where both parties have wide authority and freedom for manoeuvre. These conditions were fulfilled in Kissinger's dealings with both the Soviet Union and China. They were also fulfilled to some extent in his dealings with Le Doc Tho on Vietnam.

At that time, Nixon empowered Kissinger to act according to what the Secretary of State believed best and made him answerable only to the President himself. Nixon was disdainful of both the Congress and the press and had no qualms about putting a *fait accompli* before American institutions, especially when it came to issues which he considered vital to national security. All the more so when it came to decisions which he knew wide segments of American public opinion would applaud, regardless of what they thought of him personally.

Difficulties arose whenever Kissinger has had to deal multilaterally, as with his European allies, for example. The parties to his European talks are multiple, with non-identical interests. Furthermore, the talks are held in full view of the press and public opinion. They are submitted to the control of various institutions, agencies, and complex constitutional procedures which scrutinise every issue. This style of constrained negotiation is the very opposite to the one in which Kissinger excels.

Whenever Kissinger had to deal with more than one party at a time, whether in the case of Vietnam or in that of the Middle East after the October war, he adopted the same inflexible, basic line of selecting specific links in the conflict situation according to a preconceived plan and translating them into contractual agreements binding each party to the conflict independently. He deliberately overlooks other links in the 'conflict situation' on the pretext that no agreement can be reached on them in the immediate future. As the links he does choose to solve vary according to the interests and outlooks of the various parties, their commitments and the content and scope of their obligations also vary. In fact, the only common denominator in all contractual agreements he reaches is the fact that they are undertaken by him in his capacity as intermediary or, to be more precise, as the maestro who conducts the procedure towards a settlement according to American interests. This step-by-step approach, where Kissinger alone decides the course of events, is what he is insisting on applying in the Middle East. For him the Geneva Conference should be no more than a forum where the results of the talks he has conducted backstage are to be signed and sealed. It is precisely this procedure of tackling each link of the 'conflict situation' as a separate part that Professor Arbatov criticised as a substitute to taking security agreements collectively.

Kissinger's technique is certainly very risky. Any slip in this precarious equilibrium can bring about the collapse of the whole negotiation process. In September 1974, he himself expressed anxiety over the emergence of various crisis situations which threatened world stability, in spite of détente: inflation in the West, danger of famines in the underdeveloped world, more bottlenecks in the domain of energy. He has described the current situation as one of an exceedingly delicate equilibrium which, unless it is maintained, would plunge the world into chaos.

NOTE

1. It is worth while noting that Kissinger, who engineered the United States' détente policy, and John Foster Dulles, who engineered its policy of brinkmanship, have much in common. Both are tough negotiators who are not averse to brandishing the stick when necessary. Kissinger does not see this as incompatible with his détente policy. For instance, after the preliminary Vietnam Agreement of November 1972, the US stepped up its bombing raids on North Vietnam as never before, in the hope of making the Vietnamese negotiators more amenable.

5. Rearranging the Contradictions

Détente has been the subject of conflicting interpretations, one being that it is a new international 'order' or 'system' and another that it is, on the contrary, only 'anarchy' and 'chaos'. This chapter will attempt to set forth a coherent explanation of this phenomenon.

The transfer from Cold War to peaceful coexistence in no way implies the abolition of international contradictions which remain resistant because they involve the opposition of régimes of quite different social type, with irreconcilable interests and ideologies based on class. It would be more appropriate to say that détente was the outcome of a deliberate and conscious effort by the leaders of the capitalist and socialist worlds to 'freeze', 'isolate' or 'limit' the effects of a given set of contradictions whose individual benefit to any one party is far outweighed by their aggregate disadvantage to all. These contradictions have been 'frozen' by mutual agreement between the interested parties; the mutual commitments have been stabilised by a whole machinery of reciprocal guarantees. Nonetheless, this process does not remove the contradictions themselves; curbed, they may take unexpected form. Thus contradictions are not abolished, merely 'rearranged'.

What contradictions are to be frozen? Basically we are talking about those contradictions which are harmful to the whole human race. These go further than the divergence of interest which distinguishes national communities, social classes or collectivities grouped in a single culture, ideology or level of progress in the technical and scientific fields. As to the harm generated by these contradictions, it may come from many sources: incompatibility between levels of progress in science or technology, strains in our relationship with the natural environment or tensions in the social evolution of the human community. Let us take a few instances:

The agreements that have been made between the USSR and the US to prevent nuclear war, to limit strategic arms (the

SALT negotiations) and to halt the arms race are all efforts to 'freeze' a form of contradiction that threatens to annihilate the whole human race. In this particular case the harm lies in the fact that now the exponential growth in science and technology is not only confined to fields which benefit mankind. It has also affected the field of armament which disproportionately increases our capacity for destruction.

The agreements on scientific and technical co-operation signed by the United States and the Soviet Union have not been solely aimed at optimising the results of research and lowering costs through joint ventures, but also at avoiding the consequences of industrial pollution. Here too there is the 'freezing' of a contradiction with harmful consequences. Once more the origin of the harm lies in the present acceleration of scientific and technical progress, with the difference that this time the harm is not due to the diversion of scientific progress towards destructive ends, but is inherent in the dialectic of creative work.

The spectre of famine which already haunts many poor countries may also in the future induce the need for international agreements binding all countries of the world. These agreements would not be dictated solely by humanitarian considerations, but also by less disinterested motivation, particularly the desire to avoid the propagation of epidemics which could harm the affluent just as much as the poor, in a world where distances have been enormously reduced; and also the political aim of preventing any social convulsions which might be caused by these catastrophes. In this case the contradiction to be 'frozen' is the growing gap between developed and underdeveloped countries. But this time it is not the gains of modern technology, its 'superiority' which lies at the origin of the harm, but rather its inability to provide all mankind's needs, its impotence in rationally exploiting natural resources, the gap between the rhythm of demographic growth and men's aptitude to provide foodstuffs for themselves.

Does this imply that détente can 'freeze' one contradiction after another until all contradictions disappear? Is it a gradual transfer from the present state of 'chaos' where conflicts proliferate for want of machinery to regulate them, towards a system of nations where concord and harmony will finally prevail? In reality the category of conflicts which lend themselves to 'freezing' is extremely limited. This 'freezing' means merely a restraint applied to certain forms of the conflict, an agreement to neutralise some of the manifestations to make way for different ones. The degree of intensity may vary from one form to another, and equally the degree of harmfulness or usefulness for the interested parties. This cannot in any event imply that the contradiction itself has disappeared. For instance, to replace the arms race by economic competition between the two opposite social systems is a striking illustration of this point. In a world dominated by the balance of nuclear terror, the arms race risks destroying the whole of mankind. This is a contradiction whose manifestations are of obvious harm to both. As regards the economic competition which détente fosters, although it does not put an end to the contradiction between the two systems, it permits this contradiction to go on in such a way that it may be of advantage to both parties, inciting them to be more resolute in following a process of mutual gain, each believing from the start that he will be the beneficiary. It is thus left open to history to prove which system will survive.

Thus modes of conflict that are mutually detrimental are replaced by modes of conflict which are mutually beneficial. In reality the conflicts that are capable of being 'frozen' and transformed in this way are those that seem to menace the protagonists in equal measure. Without this feeling of common danger, the 'freezing' of conflict would be impossible. It is precisely this feeling of 'equivalence' in the perceived threat which generates the common will to seek means of pursuing the conflict in less harmful ways and leads to accommodations and accords.

The decision to control a conflict and 'freeze' it has to come from the key figures on whom the outcome of the conflict depends. These are generally heads of state or leaders of the international community. Now, for a decision to come from the 'top', there must be a situation that will convince the decision-makers that their common interest requires that the conflict take on a different form. Of course, decisions of this type imply that some restraint 'regularises' the free play of the conflicts and contradictions which hitherto had been submitted to no such restraint. This does not exclude the possibility of the resurgence of other forms of conflict, this time emanating from 'below', from the lower depths of society. These other aspects of conflict had been 'frozen' throughout the Cold War, as international polarisation tended to suppress them and absorb them. With the advent of détente, it becomes more difficult to shackle their upsurge.

Having established this we can emphasise one distinctive feature of détente which is that within the hierarchy of the international community, the contradictions which manifest themselves more actively have been displaced 'downwards' and, conversely, the contradictions liable to be 'frozen' have been displaced 'upwards'. In the Cold War the frozen conflicts were those emanating from below, which were alien to the basic issues of confrontation at the summit. Now with the depolarisation of the world, a wider spectrum of reasons of conflict is emerging with greater intensity from the depths of human society. A European illustration of this is the resurgence of regionalism.

Détente cannot suppress conflicts but instead makes the most of them by revitalising them. It has substituted more 'legitimate' confrontations for the 'forbidden' conflicts so that rather than threaten our globe with cataclysmic disaster, they become a source of renewal and enrichment. Qualitatively there is enrichment when the interplay of contradictions ends up in a 'non-zero sum game'. Instead of being a loss for all, there is a gain for all parties which can qualify as such. Quantitatively there is enrichment when released from the debilitating constraints of polarisation, and the expression of confrontation between men becomes more fecund in its diversity and multiplicity. One of the most marked features of détente is the proliferation of more or less independent actors who interact with feedback so that it has become more and more difficult to isolate one state of crisis from another.

The Middle East conflict is significant in this respect. Its protagonists are not solely limited to states (Israel, the Arab countries) but also include movements (Palestine Liberation Organisation) and even problems (the energy problem, the monetary problem, inflation, commodities, etc.). Some of these elements are geographically localisable but some are not; they intermingle and confront each other according to a much more complex cybernetical model. This is what invalidates the current thesis of strategic study centres that détente has replaced bipolarity with a multipolar international system with five or even six poles if the Arabs are now to be included. It is no longer possible to reduce poles, participants or actors to localisable entities, either geographically or otherwise. It becomes more and more difficult to enumerate the parties in a conflict, to identify a common denominator. It is therefore better to consider the movement of contradictions between these parties, whatever their nature, because the interplay of contradictions has an identifiable character even if the participants are less easy to define.

In reality détente has introduced a new element into the interplay of contradictions. For the first time in history intervention from the very summit of the international community is required to brake, control and freeze the spontaneous outbreak of certain conflicts, certain contradictions, because for the first time man has reached the threshold where the instruments of struggle he has created may terminate his very existence on the globe. Without implying their suppression, international conflicts have in this way acquired an infinitely greater complexity. Their topography is no longer confined to the map of the world's states. International agencies are no longer the only qualified bodies to find solutions. This greater diversification of conflict which disrupts the established patterns may make for confusion and disarray. This complex array of conflicts erupting from below might eventually jeopardise agreements reached at the top. We cannot escape this danger. But for some time to come we shall probably witness a chaotic situation of stalemates and convulsions which betray disequilibria. The obvious disparity of opportunity open to the participants in various conflicts will encourage this. It always requires birth pangs for the new-born to acquire the right to live; so too any new international 'order'.

6. Détente and the Middle East — Is Washington Looking Eastwards?

Détente has brought about some amount of change in US attitudes towards the Middle East. Various interpretations of its significance and scope are put forward. The change was hinted at in Arnaud de Borchgrave's *Newsweek* article probing Kissinger's views six months before the October war, took a more concrete shape with the outbreak of the war, and found full expression with Kissinger's active diplomacy ever since.

With the end of the Cold War, Europe is no longer the most volatile and sensitive region in the world. Neither is the Far East as explosive as it was at the time the United States followed a policy of circumscribing China with a succession of limited wars stretching from Korea in the north to Vietnam in the south. Tension relaxed with the US *rapprochement* with China, with US withdrawal from Vietnam, and since the signing of the Paris Vietnam Agreement in 1973. The only hot point with no solution in view in the years prior to the October war was the Middle East. In spite of an apparent lull, defined as 'no-war, no-peace', the Middle East crisis carried the greatest threat to the new climate of détente. The Middle East has traditionally occupied a marginal position in US global strategy. They could not afford to ignore it completely — after all, the underbelly of the Soviet Union could not be overlooked; the vacuum was filled to the extent that a network of military alliances was stretched to the Middle East, and Israel acquired growing importance in the US strategy — to counter the developing Arab liberation movement and to guarantee a permanent western outpost at this strategic crossroads intersected by the vital artery of the Suez Canal.

But the United States never missed a chance to muscle in on the region. It tried to turn the collapse of French and British colonialism to its advantage, and sought to fill the vacuum by more insidious means of penetration, like the Eisenhower Doctrine. When this Doctrine was rejected by the maturing Arab liberation movement, America's reliance on Israel increased. In 1967 Israel managed to inflict an unparalleled military disaster on the Arabs and to portray Soviet military assistance to the progressive Arab régimes as being inadequate in face of superior American-Israeli logistics. Thanks to Israel, the United States was able to curb the Arab liberation movement, to undermine Nasser's image and to denigrate the achievements of the '52 Revolution without sacrificing one American soldier in the process, unlike the heavy price it paid in Vietnam. At the same time, the United States built other strongholds for itself in the region, especially Saudi Arabia and Iran, whose importance grew in proportion to the growing importance of oil.

The United States could no longer base its relations on the previous rationale of complete polarisation, which it had not only accepted but actively nourished. It could no longer reconcile between total bias to Israel, antagonism for the Arab countries subjected to Israeli occupation, and maintaining solid relations with the Arab oil-producing countries. World polarisation was no longer a justification or a stimulus for regional polarisation which could impede understanding between Arab countries with different social systems, especially now that the Middle East crisis was still locked in an impasse and new reasons for reconciliation between them had emerged.

Although Europe was not as sensitive and volatile as it was before détente, it still occupied a key position in US global strategy. In this new situation, American leverage on Europe came to depend more on issues outside Europe like the Middle East. Ensuring her interests in a multipolar world did not entail only strengthening the western alliance in face of the socialist camp, but also consolidating her own position *vis-à-vis* her European allies and deterring any attempt on their part to assert themselves, in the name of European security, at the expense of the Atlantic alliance. Not all western countries are equally dependent on Arab oil, which is basic for Europe and Japan but still only marginal for the United States. Furthermore, any increase in the price of oil is to the advantage of the major oil companies, which are mainly American. This situation presented the United States with a golden opportunity to control not only the energy crisis, but also the destinies of other industrialised western countries by controlling the sources of oil. And, finally, not only is the United States the western country which is least dependent on Arab oil, but also the one most capable of exerting leverage on Israel. The October war proved the fallacy of Israel's contention that it is 'independent' of America. And it raised another question: to what extent could the United States be 'independent' of Israel's pressure lobbies?

For the first time a situation arose placing the United States before a possible choice of two policies: either to pursue its traditional policy of complete alignment with Israel, disregarding the new factors which have emerged since détente, or to follow a new policy which could depart to a certain extent from Israel's own goals, but which would realise various advantages for the US. The first of these advantages would be to turn the oil weapon to its own account, and to use it against Europe and Japan, both economically and politically.

Economically, the United States would control the price of industrial products exported by Europe and Japan by controlling oil prices, which would be raised or lowered according to the US's competitive interests in world markets. This control could eventually provide leverage to regulate inflation and handle the monetary problems. And, more important, politically, it would put a stop to all attempts by western countries to dispute its unchallenged leadership. To retain its superpower status, the United States must prove its ability to achieve what others cannot. It must prove its ability to control the energy crisis. This in turn entails controlling the Middle East crisis and using the energy crisis as a lever. Furthermore, accumulation of Arab assets in world banks is a link connecting the oil-producing countries to the world capitalist economy, and by controlling the oil weapon, the United States transforms these countries into a Trojan Horse which can be used to divide the Third World.

The Middle East Crisis and the Energy Crisis

But for the United States to control the oil weapon, oil should no longer be a function of the Middle East crisis. The Middle East crisis should become a function of the oil issue, i.e. American intervention in the Middle East crisis will be determined by its interest *vis-à-vis* the energy crisis.

A number of important issues stem from this. Foremost

among them is that the United States is likely to shift the focal point from Palestine, heart of the Arab-Israeli conflict, eastwards to the Gulf region, where conflicting strategies are expected to wrestle for control of the main reservoirs of world oil. Here a number of patterns of confrontation can be anticipated:

Pattern 'A' would pit those countries friendly to the United States, headed by Saudi Arabia and Iran, against the progressive or non-aligned countries friendly to the Soviet Union, like Iraq, South Yemen, Syria, Afghanistan and India.[1] This pattern is likely to link the energy crisis to regional crises, not only to the Middle East crisis, but possibly stretching to the still unsolved crises in the Indian sub-continent as well as to the volatile situation on both shores south of the Red Sea. An added complication is the growing importance of the sea itself in the strategies of the great powers (most of the hot points overlook the Red Sea and the Indian Ocean), especially after the re-opening of the Suez Canal.

Even if we assume that since détente summit talks could prevent regional conflicts from getting out of hand and directly involving the superpowers, this is not the case with Pattern 'B'. This pattern includes only those countries friendly to the United States, specifically Saudi Arabia and Iran. Thanks to oil revenues, both countries have built up enormous wealth in a short span of time. Both aspire to the leading role in the Gulf. They are separated only by a group of emirates, newcomers to oil wealth, with fragile institutions and pending border problems. There is an obvious lag between the respective ability of the two 'regional superpowers' to modernise. Iran has the infrastructure which would allow it to develop at a faster rate than Saudi Arabia, and is consequently better placed to achieve hegemony over the Gulf. On the other hand, Saudi Arabia and the emirates have Arabism in common. In the past, Iranis slipped into the emirates in search of a living. Will this result in a phenomenon similar to Jewish infiltration into Palestine? Will an Irani settler presence gradually build up in the Gulf states? Iran has already occupied three Arab islands at the mouth of the Gulf. What next?

For the United States these factors are additional incentives for a reappraisal of its strategy and for shifting its attentions to the Gulf. But besides incentives there are also deterrents. The

United States might be able to prevent a conflict between Saudi Arabia and Iran from escalating, but cannot intervene with the same efficacy to cope with Palestinian activities in the Gulf. American decision-makers are accustomed to dealing with the lobby groups of the Jewish Diaspora, but are not yet familiar with the need to reckon with the Palestinian Diaspora, which is not represented in Congress or articulate in the press, but is a 'presence' dispersed throughout the Arab oil-producing countries, especially in the Gulf. The Americans may not see any threat in this presence if it is confined to the Palestinians who constitute the backbone of oil technocracy in the Arabian peninsula. But they will certainly perceive a deadly menace if they realise that the children of these technocrats could constitute an important auxiliary for the 'rejectionist' front. The fathers might be cowed by their responsibilities and lured by their high pay, but the sons form an intelligentsia which could be attracted by the logic of the rejectionists if the Palestinian problem finds no solution and the contrast between the hell of the refugee camps and the accumulation of fabulous wealth on the peninsula becomes more stark. Blowing up oil installations or mining the Hormouz Straits at the mouth of the Gulf is scarcely more difficult than hijacking a Jumbo jet.

This mode of behaviour is not alien to the CIA, which has hinted that it would not hestitate to adopt *fedayeen* techniques to coerce and blackmail recalcitrant Arab sheikhs rebelling against Washington's diktats. Thus the weapons of the rejections are now acknowledged by the United States to be an integral part of the political game and which, though directed against it, it is not averse to using.

Kissinger's Dilemmas

Kissinger seems to have been aware of this quite early in the day. It may have been why he favoured 'shock therapy' six months prior to the October war, as a short cut to a new strategy. His active diplomacy as soon as the war broke out, followed by the rapid disengagement on both the Egyptian and Syrian fronts, leave one with the impression that the architect of American diplomacy was implementing, step by step, a previously conceived scenario. Thus the United States was required to become a 'friend' of all countries in the region, without exception, in a manner that would guarantee

American control of both the energy crisis and the Middle East crisis.

But this in turn is bound to pose a number of dilemmas: How much can the United States 'give' the Arabs without upsetting Israel? How can it reconcile between not keeping the Soviets 'out' of an agreement and not allowing them to take active part in the decision-making? How to strike the right balance in the tempo of the settlement, which should not be allowed to forge ahead too quickly as this would allow forces which the United States cannot control to emerge, nor to move too slowly as this would let some of the threads slip from its grasp? With regard to Europe, a delicate balance must be maintained between preserving the western alliance and using the Middle East crisis, through the oil issue, as a sword of Damocles.

Walking tightropes of this kind is Kissinger's forte. However, US policy has never been determined in terms of an abstract global strategy but by various pressure groups, each representing one partial interest or another. The United States' overall strategy is simply the sum total of these interests.

At one point Kissinger seemed to rise above the conflicting pressure groups, and to introduce a foreign policy based on rationality. This impression was further confirmed when Nixon appointed Kissinger Secretary of State in addition to his previous post as national security adviser. But this impression was an illusion created by Kissinger's personal abilities. In his second term in office, a unique relationship developed between the President and his Secretary of State for, alone among the members of his immediate entourage, Kissinger remained unsoiled by Watergate. Through him Nixon hoped to achieve startling successes for his foreign policy to offset his dwindling assets at home.

But the situation was bound to change after Nixon's resignation. The Ford-Kissinger duo is not the Nixon-Kissinger duo. Nixon's relations with Congress had reached an all-time low. Kissinger's foreign policy, especially as regards the Middle East, was not looked upon as serving US global strategy but, rather, as protecting Nixon from indictment. Since the October war Kissinger's policy towards the Arab-Israeli conflict has not been confined to unconditional support for Israel, but has also striven to win the confidence of the Arabs, leading to questions in Congress by the Jewish lobby.

Unlike Nixon, Ford cannot challenge Congress. However powerful the Israeli lobby may be, it is not all-powerful. But in coalition with a number of other lobbies, it can acquire a significant weight. Most prominent of these is the anti-détente lobby, led by Senator Jackson, who is sceptical of Kissinger's policies in general. Another is the violently anti-Communist trade union lobby. In the face of this coalition there is no effective Arab lobby, for while American oil corporations have influential representatives in Congress, they have no joint policy *vis-à-vis* Arab demands, nor is there a consensus on how best to deal with the Arab oil-producing countries. Some contend that the stick rather than the carrot would be more effective in guaranteeing the corporations' long-term interests.

Israel is aware of these new loopholes in Kissinger's diplomacy, which no longer has the same credibility for it and, consequently, for the other parties. Kissinger's claim that America holds all the keys to a peaceful solution is now questionable. In the disengagement talks on both the Sinai and Golan fronts, Kissinger was at his best; it is doubtful whether he can carry off a repeat performance. For his successes were on procedural aspects rather than on the basic issues. The closer one gets to these basic issues the more difficult it will become for American diplomacy to devise formulations acceptable to all parties. Kissinger himself is aware of this and does not hesitate to use the precarious situation as a lever to impose his ideas, intimating that the alternative to his policy would be total chaos.

NOTE

1. This classification of mid-eastern countries has become less marked since Kissinger's diplomacy has succeeded in normalising the US's relations with most of these countries.

7. Détente and the Middle East — Is Moscow Looking Westwards?

In April 1974, one of the last remaining bastions of European colonialism in the south-western tip of Europe collapsed when a military *coup* took over in Portugal. Another bastion fell in the south-eastern tip of Europe with the downfall of the military junta in Greece. In both cases, anti-fascists of all shades, including the Communists, regained their freedom after long years of persecution. Between these two furthermost points on Europe's southern flank, events are moving fast and the left is gaining ground.

In Italy there is a widespread conviction that there can be no stability without Communist participation in government. In France, the Socialist-Communist Union of the left failed to bring its candidate, Francois Mitterand, to the Elysee by a 1 per cent margin of votes. And Spanish Communist Party General Secretary Santiago Carrillo secretly receives in his Paris exile representatives of the whole political gamut in Spain. Will the Soviet Union's keenness on maintaining this momentum of the left in south Europe affect its Middle East policy? If Israel or the US were to stage a showdown in the Middle East, would the Soviet Union, as certain western analysts contend, sidestep the challenge to avoid the dilemma of having to choose between friendship with the Arabs and the fruits of détente in Europe?

The USSR's relationship with certain Arab countries was marked by a seemingly strange feature: co-operation between Egypt and the Soviet Union at times exceeded the co-operation with states belonging to the socialist community. This relationship between the USSR and Egypt was described as one of 'friendship'. Perhaps the word friendship in the political idiom needs a more accurate definition, but obviously it does not base mutual commitments on common ideological grounds. In any case, the relationship is looser than relations within the socialist community, based on 'proletarian internationalism'. How to explain that on the *practical* level the USSR's relations

55

with Egypt have at times attained a level *above* that of its relations with the socialist community while on the *principled* level they have always remained *below?* Was this due to shortcomings in the implementation of 'proletarian internationalism'? It is true that there are contradictions between the socialist states that can attain a degree of downright antagonism, the Sino-Soviet dispute being a glaring example. Neither is it excluded that clearly divergent points of view can emerge between the Soviet Union and some of the European Communist parties, especially if any of them participate in government. Many of these parties did not conceal their disapproval of Soviet intervention in Czechoslovakia. The core of the argument was: should each Communist party adapt to the requirement of the union of all national forces in the struggle for socialism, or should each party give precedence to the cohesion of the socialist community, even if this should temporarily produce frictions among the national forces? This argument has not been resolved yet. These facts however do not explain why Soviet-Egyptian friendship attained such a scope.

Soviet-Egyptian Friendship

The Soviet-Egyptian friendship was born and grew in the climate of harsh confrontation against a common enemy: imperialism in general and US imperialism in particular, at a time when the spectre of the Cold War had not yet been laid to rest. The relationship was that of a socialist state with an independent national state, state power in each having a different class content. However, the conditions in which the emerging national states achieved independence and resisted imperialism's attempts to regain its influence were bound to promote their *rapprochement* with the socialist community, especially with the tense international climate, even if the newly emerged national leaders were keen on asserting their ideological identity at the same time that they sought this *rapprochement.* The Soviet Union welcomed this growing relationship not only because it activated national liberation movements and strengthened the young national states, but also because it favoured the security of the Soviet Union itself, loosened imperialism's grip over the Third World, undermined its ability to encircle the socialist camp, deterred its attempts to oppose it by war, isolated imperialism's most aggressive circles and promoted a more balanced world equilibrium of force, liable to bring the Cold War to an end and pave the way to peaceful coexistence and détente.

The strategic position of the Middle East within this global Soviet strategy was one of particular importance, not only because of its geographical location on the underbelly of the Soviet Union but also because of the nationalistic fermentation in most of its countries, polarised around the acute conflict between Israel and the Arabs. In this context, Egypt was a key state because of its standing in the Arab world and also because its 1952 Revolution had served as an impetus to the whole Third World.

However, this strategy came up against a number of complex issues following Egypt's military defeat in 1967. On the one hand the defeat upgraded the relationship, while on the other it brought forth latent problems which were bound to drive the two sides apart.

Before June 1967 both sides were agreed that the problem of social change in Egypt had top priority once the national problem had been solved in its essence. The Soviets saw the soundness in the Egyptian revolution's basic line regardless of their difference in approach. But things changed after June 1967, and the national problem rose once again to the fore. For Egypt, 'recovering the occupied territories' and 'removing the consequences of the aggression' acquired top priority. The Soviet Union stood fast by Egypt's side in the dark days following the defeat. It in no way underrated the importance of the national problem. On the contrary, its massive arms shipments to Egypt immediately after the defeat were of vital importance in creating favourable conditions for Arab resistance. However, the seeds of a divergence in outlook were sown with the very first moment of the Israeli aggression. If it was to be expected that the Soviet approach to resolving the 'national' problem would be from the angle of 'social change', it was equally to be expected that for the Egyptian leadership the problem of 'social change' should be adapted to the requirements of the 'national' problem.

For the Soviets, making the problem of 'social change' the point of departure meant adhering to the course of the 1952 Revolution, deepening and widening the revolutionary process, i.e. consolidating the progressive Arab régimes, extending them to a greater number of Arab countries, and strengthening Arab fighting capability. From this angle, the Soviets saw the re-emergence of the national problem (removing the consequences of the aggression) as a link in the Arab liberation movement. Even if it might require a long process of struggle, a whole strategic stage, even if it were particularly violent and bitter, it was still nevertheless one of these links and in itself contained no justification to depart from the basic objectives. For the Soviets, the key to speeding up this process did not lie in sticking to the slogan of destroying Israel, but in affecting the class structures in favour of progressive forces in the region and to expose class forces which supported the aggression, which accepted it as a *fait accompli* or which exacerbated it still more, whether these forces were the ruling Zionist circles in Israel or Arab reactionary forces with their equally strong links with imperialism. The Soviet outlook did not rule out striving for a *rapprochement* between all left and democratic forces in the region against those having a vested interest in the continuation and extension of the aggression, especially the ruling circles in Israel.

As for the Egyptian stand, giving the 'national' problem precedence over the problem of 'social change' was bound to set the removal of aggression within the framework of Pan-Arab nationalism. This acquired complex new dimensions as it came to be believed that the source of Arab power was not restricted to the Arab revolution — exclusively centred round the explosive Palestinian revolution — but extended also to Arab oil wealth. This stand held that the use of oil as a weapon should not be discarded, even if this entailed overtures to Arab oil-producing countries. Most of these countries had conservative régimes, so the problem of progressive 'social change' was shelved.

The disparity between the two stands remained covert in the immediate aftermath of the 1967 war, when the Soviet Union and the socialist community were alone in supplying the progressive Arab régimes which had been exposed to aggression, with arms and economic and political assistance. This assistance was vital in limiting the defeat to its military aspect, making it one lost battle in a long confrontation of many links. However, as time passed and no tangible results were forthcoming, the points of disparity began to overshadow the points of agreement. When Sadat's 'year of decision' flopped, Cairo complained that it was short of the arms needed to resume fighting and to protect the Nile valley from Israel's raids in depth. In private talk the Soviets made no secret of their apprehension that the internal front was not geared for a battle requiring mass mobilisation. Certainly also they did not want their military equipment to be the subject of western gloating as it was after the 1967 defeat.

Thus the wheel was set in motion. To the same extent that Cairo felt that Soviet military assistance could not revive a military solution, it felt the need to probe a political one. Obviously a political solution entailed a dialogue with the West, including the United States. Not that the Soviets had any objection in principle to a probe of the chances for a political solution — in fact, they made no secret of their preference for this course of action. The reservation they may have held was that such a dialogue would not be evenly matched if the Soviet Union did not take part as a counterbalance to the United States and its expected attempts to manipulate the crisis to the detriment of the Arab liberation movement.

A spoke in the wheel was the military *coup* against Numeiry in the Sudan. It was a milestone at this delicate moment, signalling the limitations of 'friendship'. The Soviets apparently did express reservations on the *coup*, at least according to what purported to be minutes of the discussions between the Soviet Communist Party and the Syrian Communist Party over a split which had affected the latter's ranks in 1972, and which were 'leaked out' to the Beirut press. In the event, these reservations were never voiced outside Communist inter-party discussions. But the Soviet leadership must have felt that Cairo's attitude to the *coup* and to the Sudanese Communist Party placed them in an awkward position *vis-à-vis* internal public opinion and the world Communist movement.

Another more important development was the advent of détente, which promised to sanction, for the first time, peaceful coexistence between the two greatest powers on earth. Although this development in itself does not justify the assumption that either of the two sides would abandon its principles, the fact that a *rapprochement* occurred when the Middle East crisis had reached a total impasse gave rise to deep unease in Cairo.

Cairo's reaction to the first Soviet-American summit in May 1972 was to bring the presence of Soviet military experts to an end. Cairo felt that Soviet strategy had placed *rapprochement* with the US, détente and peaceful coexistence, before the Arab liberation movement, and that the Soviet Union was not prepared to upgrade its military assistance to Egypt to the extent of endangering mutual confidence with the United States. Cairo pointed to the slackening in arms supplies, the reluctance to meet Cairo's requests for specific sophisticated weapons, as well as to the new policy of allowing large numbers of Soviet Jews to emigrate to Israel, a step which contradicted the traditional reluctance of the Soviet Union to respond to pressures for emigration of Soviet citizens.

There seems to be no doubt that a certain reversal in priorities had in fact occurred. Perhaps the Soviets gave priority to a breakthrough towards the Third World and, specifically the Arab liberation movement, at a time when the Cold War menace was acute, as a means to contain imperialism by hitting it in its rear. This might explain the privileged status of progressive Arab regimes in Soviet aid programmes, exceeding interstate co-operation within the socialist community. But as soon as imperialism's thrust slackened and an opportunity arose to end the Cold War and to build a new relationship with the West — and the US in particular — it is obvious that Soviet strategy gave priority to sustaining this achievement. This occured when the Middle East crisis seemed completely deadlocked before the October war and chances of achieving tangible results in liquidating the vestiges of the Cold War with the US and the West appeared more likely than those of liquidating the consequences of the hot war in the Middle East. The Soviets have always maintained that their priorities are not determined erratically but according to what best responds to the struggle the peoples themselves undertake for the fulfilment of their aims.

A Three-Party Game

And so Cairo was openly worried before the October war because of the Soviet-American *rapprochement*. Similarly, the Soviets must have felt uneasy after the October war by Egyptian-American *rapprochement*. Why should the *rapprochement* of each side with the United States cast a shadow over Soviet-Egyptian relations?

Soviet-Egyptian friendship was founded on anti-imperialism. It began when the Cold War had not yet thawed out. Even if the acute polarisation at that time brought them together, the concept of anti-imperialism need not have meant the same thing for the two sides. The leadership of the 1952 Revolution grasped the concept of imperialism through a process passing from the 'particular' to the 'general'. The imperialist threat to national independence came to be felt through the Israeli challenge and the experience of the Free Officers in the Palestine war of 1948. The Soviet Union's assistance to Egypt in its struggle against Israel, on the other hand, reflected a passing from the 'general' to the 'particular' — from an outlook on imperialism as a complex world phenomenon, to identifying Israel's aggressive policy towards the Arab liberation movement as one specific facet of this phenomenon. This disparity in approach explains why the Soviet leaders submitted the goal of 'removing the consequences of the aggression' (specific Middle East issue) to the problem of 'social change' (against imperialism in general) and why the Egyptian leadership submitted the problem of 'social change' (a world anti-imperialism stand) to the goal of 'removing the consequences of the aggression' (the specific national issue that brought about its awareness of the phenomenon of imperialism).

As long as global polarisation remained acute, as long as both sides were exposed to the onslaught of imperialism which took various openly aggresive forms, neither side could afford to indulge in these differences. In fact, neither side differentiated between imperialism as a world phenomenon and the American state, which was looked upon by both as the major imperialist state with whom each had limited and tense relations.

With the effect of détente, the Soviet Union did not change its assessment of imperialism, but was faced with the necessity of distinguishing between imperialism and the US. Imperialist America was no longer an impediment to the Soviet Union's dealings with the American state.

With the outbreak of the October war and with Kissinger's emergence on the Middle East scene, Egyptian-American relations developed and Egypt too was faced with the necessity of distinguishing between its attitude to imperialism on the one hand and to the American state on the other.

Both sides agree that the US is an indispensable party to a settlement in the Middle East crisis. That the Soviets do not deny this is attested to by Kissinger's talks in Moscow during the October war and by their acknowledgement that the US must be a party to the Geneva Conference. Both sides also concure that détente does not mean the disappearance of world conflicts nor the fading away of imperialism. However, neither side expects their relationship to develop further on the basis of deeper hostility towards the US as a state or with any other western state or group of states.

A Need for Basing Relations on New Grounds

Thus a new foundation for Soviet-Egyptian friendship must be laid. All previous misunderstandings must be cleared up, for no agreement is likely if differences continue to be dismissed. Otherwise differences will grow deeper[1] and will acquire subjective connotations beyond their objective dimensions, such as Egypt's contention that détente meant 'entente' and an 'embrace' between the two superpowers, or its reading of the clause on 'military relaxation in the Middle East' in the first Brezhnev-Nixon summit as a decision to be implemented before a settlement is reached. The Soviets saw reasons for apprehension in these contentions which raised question marks in their mind as to whether the trust Egypt gave to Kissinger was justified, and whether he should alone hold all the strings of a settlement.

During a trip to the USSR just before the October war, I met a number of Soviet officials and experts in various fields, all of whom expressed the view that the Soviet Union's relations with the Arabs and Egypt should not be evaluated as inversely proportionate to its relations with the United States. They held that imperialism and Zionism are the main beneficiaries of tension in international relations.

For the Soviets there is no contradiction between peaceful coexistence and development of the national liberation movement. They consider the two tasks complementary. By allowing negotiations and not just confrontation with the US, détente can curb aggression, including Israeli aggression, more effectively and further promote the Arab liberation movement.

On the other hand, every new accomplishment of the liberation movement curtails imperialism and builds détente and peaceful coexistence on firm foundations.

The fact remains that Egypt was able to wage the October war thanks to the arms it received from the Soviet Union even after the assignment of Soviet experts in Egypt was terminated. These arms supplies proved that though the Soviet Union is keen on détente and on improving its relations with the United States, it will not accept a deterioration in its relations with the Arab liberation movement, nor concede that the assets built through the years of Arab-Soviet friendship are bound to be lost.

Soviet-Egyptian friendship is not confined to the past. It has an obvious role to play in handling the achievements of the October war to impose a just peace. Only force is effective in regaining what was seized by force. Unless the Arabs continue to use force, or to manifest the fact that they do possess this force, in military terms or otherwise, there is no chance of achieving the Arab hope for a settlement based on a just peace. The military component here is indispensable. And whatever can be said about the Soviet Union holding back the arms necessary to replenish the Egyptian aresenal we cannot reasonably expect western countries or the US to supplant the Soviet Union in this respect. Certain western countries may be interested in providing arms to Egypt as a way to stabilise their balance of payments, or to cover in part the increased cost of Arab oil. However, these countries cannot provide Egypt with arms at the same level of sophistication as those which the US supplies to Israel. Nor can they meet all Egypt's demands for sophisticated arms. Its decision to diversify its sources of arms obviously means that it no longer wishes to depend on Soviet arms alone. But it certainly cannot mean that it plans to do without Soviet arms, because the Egyptian army has been trained on them for two decades and cannot replace them by western arms overnight — if only for technical reasons.

Soviet-Egyptian friendship also has a role to play in future Egyptian economic development. This development has been exposed to economic and industrial bottlenecks because of defence priorities. The stability of Egypt's development cannot depend only or essentially on the economic 'open-door policy' or on assistance and investments from the West or the Arab oil-producing countries. Inflation has an obvious tendency to make the weaker partners carry its burden. Egypt can only contain the effects of instability by preserving strong relations with the socialist community.

However keen the Soviet Union may be to promote the momentum of democracy in Europe and to consolidate détente, it will not realise this by turning its back on the Middle East and leaving it prey to the US and Israel. There is no contradiction between the Soviet Union's keenness on promoting détente in Europe and opposing attempts by the US and Israel to bring the situation in the Middle East to the brink. The Soviet Union, like the United States, is aware that the Arab-Israel conflict is *the* central question in international relations; the fate of détente will be decided across the battle lines drawn between Israel and her Arab neighbours.

NOTE

1. Since this book was written the Egyptian-Soviet Friendship Treaty, signed after Sadat took full power in May 1971 by removing the Ali Sabry group, was unilaterally abrogated by Egypt on 14 March 1976.

PART III: WHITHER THE MIDDLE EAST?

8. And if a Settlement is Reached?

What shape will the Middle East take after a 'just and permanent peace': what will happen after the guns fall silent? Among Arabs, the topic is taboo, condemned as a notion by the bulk of public opinion, as well as by most of the intelligentsia. It is condemned because there is a deep-rooted conviction in the Arab psyche that the only conceivable settlement would entail complete surrender to Israel's strategy, total submission to the Zionist design.

Yet the question of peace is now set as an overt and pressing goal, not as a diplomatic ploy, or a tactical manoeuvre in the strategy of eliminating Israel. Proof that this is now a genuine aim lies in the fact that it has become the basis for binding international commitments by the Arabs, commitments which cannot be easily revoked or ignored. Even if peace is not a prerequisite for the stabilisation and development of Arab-Soviet relations, it is definitely a condition for the development of Arab-American relations and for a fruitful dialogue with the European Common Market. But as long as the settlement with Israel and the future of peace in the region are not embodied in a clearly defined vision, Israel will never admit that the Arab goal is genuine; it will continue to cast doubts on the sincerity of their overtures and maintain that the Arab position is basically unchanged.

The Arab-Israeli conflict is the pivot around which all developments in the region have revolved since the foundation of Israel. In fact, as we have mentioned, the history of Egypt over the last quarter of a century has been organically linked to the creation of Israel. There is a correlation between Egypt's revolution on the night of 23 July 1952 and Israel's creation on 15 May 1948. What triggered the Free Officers movement was the humiliation suffered by the Egyptian Army in the first Palestine war. Ever since then Israel has never been absent from the vicissitudes of the Egyptian Revolution. This also applies to a large number of Arab countries.

Any attempt at this point to probe the future of Egypt or the Arab world must take the question of Israel into account. Considerations of time are irrelevant. Any forecast must take the crisis to some kind of conclusion, some kind of settlement, some day.

The well know futurologist, Herman Kahn, selects as the three most relevant options in making any forecast: the 'best' (overcoming the crisis and achieving peace), the 'worst' (eruption of a fifth war), and what he considers the 'least likely' (the continuation of what is in this case the 'no-war, no-peace', 'no-victory, no-defeat' situation). This is a facile logic because the 'best' and 'worst' could interchange positions. The outbreak of a fifth war (according to Kahn the 'worst' possibility) might be how the 'continuation of the stalemate' could be broken and peace achieved (considered the 'best' possibility). By the same token the opposite is also true. Thus peace (the 'best' possibility) could result in what the Arabs apprehend as the 'worst': capitulation to the Israeli strategy and surrender to the Zionist design.

Assuming that the road to peace — be it long or short — may include a fifth, sixth, or even a seventh war, we must ask ourselves what such wars can achieve. Even if we suppose that a new war might result in a sweeping victory for Israel, it will not invalidate the important question which a retired Israeli general, Mattetyahu Peled, raised just before the cease-fire was concluded. Reflecting the concern of the more far-sighted members of the Israeli military establishment, he asked: 'Suppose 35 million Egyptians surrendered, what would a small nation like Israel do with them?' He then asked whether it was the Zionist objective to occupy Arab lands and systematically to destroy their economies? Who would supply Israel with the wherewithal to do so? This corroborates Sadat's statement that there can be no military solution to the Middle East crisis. On the other hand, the crisis has attained such dangerous dimensions that 'no solution' is now also untenable. *Some sort* of settlement is inevitable. Israel envisages only a post-settlement future, deliberately disregarding the question of how such a settlement could be reached. The Arabs visualise only a pre-settlement future, and ignore in their turn what the implications of reaching a settlement would be. This attitude will not protect the Arabs from the hazards of a settlement, but will only serve to cloud their vision. It is therefore imperative to consider all the possible options.

What Does a Settlement Mean?

A settlement will not mean a cancelling of contradictions: this is clear from all the major settlements which have been reached since the onset of détente. To satisfy all parties concerned, a settlement between the Arabs and Israel will have to be modelled on the same lines. The settlement will indicate that the Middle East crisis will have entered the détente era and that it will have overcome the problem of absolute polarisation which characterised the Cold War, the complete absence of communication between the principals in the dispute and the lack of any common measure between them.

Thus the settlement is not a cancelling of contradictions but a deliberate rearrangement of contradictions with an aim of isolating and 'freezing' those contradictions considered more detrimental to all than beneficial to any. The settlement means formulating explicit and implicit agreements to halt the repeated resort to war. This means setting up a network of mutual guarantees based on sanctions and incentives, to encourage all parties to make the settlement an irreversible process.

Obviously this does not mean that the conflict will end, but only that it will acquire manifestly different forms. Most prominent among them will be a proliferation of relatively independent and distinct players who can no longer be assimilated into the previous polarised form of conflict, with its limited number of main actors. However complex the conflict appeared, however numerous the different approaches to the problem (social, ideological, religious, ethnic) this diversity was absorbed within a rather simple pattern determined by the basic confrontation. The various differences and disparities, actual or potential, were screened, repressed, or delayed until the main battle should be over, giving rise to slogans like: 'the voice of the battle must drown any other', the 'need to preserve national unity', the 'cohesion of the internal front', etc.

The predominant contradiction for the principals was the 'national' contradiction. The sovereignty of the Arab countries neighbouring Israel was violated by Israel's occupation of chunks of their national territory, while the Palestinian people suffered from the violation of their very existence, as a people belonging to a nation and rooted in a land. The Israelis felt that the Arabs' hostility threatened the very foundations of the Zionist design to establish a national homeland for the Jews in Palestine. Hence the conflicting parties were limited in number: the Arab states on one side, Israel on the other. In the course of the conflict the distinct identity of the Palestinian people emerged.

Even the global context of the conflict in the previous polarised international situation was characterised by a rather simple pattern. Different western countries used Israel as a weapon against the burgeoning Arab liberation movement: Britain and France after Egypt nationalised the Suez Canal, the US in a later period. As for Federal Germany, its massive arms shipments to Israel were not simply in expiation for Nazi crimes against the Jews: after all, Israel does not represent all Jews in the world, nor even all those who were subjected to Nazi persecution. However the Arabs felt the sophisticated arms which Bonn supplied to Israel were less to serve the latter's security than to serve its all-out attack against the Arabs in the 1967 war. On the other side, the socialist countries upheld Arab rights. Although their ideological stand was obviously not identical to that of the Arabs, they have constantly emphasised what is common to them both in aims and interest, notably the Arab aim of liquidating all traces of the aggression and recovering occupied territories.

Anatomy of the Crisis

With the emergence of the possibility of a settlement the pattern of the confrontation becomes less simple. No longer does the national contradiction overshadow all others, because the settlement means establishing 'secure and recognised national borders' for all the conflicting parties. This allows the possibility of much greater internal discussion and dispute within the two sides.

We have already mentioned that a 'struggle' between hawks and doves emerged in Israel after the October war. This struggle was blurred when the hawks were in the ascendancy. Also, after the onset of détente, Egypt had no objection to 'opening' in various directions. Several other Arab countries which were exposed to the aggression are following in Egypt's footsteps. An economic opening on the West means an affiliation to world capitalism. This affiliation was accompanied by a reconciliation with the conservative Arab regimes, whose oil revenues make them a prominent feature of world capitalism. Naturally with this opening towards world capitalism, the differences between political trends within Arab countries, which include parties committed to socialism, become more acute.

All this would suggest that future characteristics of conflict in the region will follow a different pattern.

In the past, the contradictions between the conflicting parties could be described as 'vertical' contradictions. By this we mean 'national' contradictions, separating the countries involved in the conflict geographically, with Israel on one side, the Arab countries on the other. Superimposed on these 'vertical' contradictions emerged 'horizontal' contradictions, which separate the various strata within the countries participating in the conflict. The 'hoirizontal' contradictions are mainly social contradictions and now rival 'vertical' contradictions in acuteness and importance. All social contradictions are, according to our definition, 'horizontal' because they are contradictions between different strata within one society, some of which belong to the upper echelons of society, others to the working classes at the base of society.

But not all 'horizontal' contradictions are social contradictions. For instance, the contradiction between doves and hawks in Israel does not represent a social contradiction, but rather a difference in outlook within similar social classes all embracing the philosophy of Zionism; they have different appraisals of Israel's basic interests and strategy. A basic social contradiction will not take hold in Israel before the emergence of the contradiction between pro-Zionism and anti-Zionism. So far this contradiction has had little impact because of the limited size and influence of non-Zionist forces.

It is clear that the map of contradictions in the region has become more complex since the October war, with the onset of détente and the opportunity for a settlement. No longer does it reflect a relatively simple pattern based on 'vertical' contradictions alone, but on the complex interplay of two distinct sets of contradictions: the initial set of 'vertical' contradictions *between* the principals to the dispute, and a new set of 'horizontal' contradictions *within* each of the principals. Moreover, a *rapprochement* between similar social trends among the protagonists is no longer checked by the acuteness of the 'vertical' contradiction alone. There is at least one point of agreement between the swelling ranks of advocates of an 'open-door policy' towards the United States in the Arab world and the rulers of Israel: that of having American diplomacy as the key figure in the peace-making process.

Thus two distinct sets of contradictions within the region overlap and intertwine. When the conflict is intensified, when tension rises or armed clashes break out, or when a full-scale war erupts, the 'vertical' comes to the fore. But this does not imply the disappearance of the 'horizontal'. They may subside temporarily but will not disappear altogether.

Although the intensification of the conflict will indicate the emergence of polarisation once again, it will only be polarisation on the regional level between the direct protagonists. It will not attain global dimensions which would reverse the world tendency towards détente. True, the situation might get out of hand, even to the extent of a nuclear confrontation, but this possibility is receding further the more international mutual commitments make détente an irreversible process.

No matter how acute the 'vertical' becomes again, the set of 'horizontal' will not disappear completely. The coexistence of the two sets of contradictions has become an irreversible process. It will go on all through the period in which the settlement is to be achieved, and with the gathering of momentum towards a settlement, the 'horizontal' contradictions will come to the fore. But the 'vertical' will not disappear, from the formal point of view at least, until a settlement is achieved and peace attained in the region.

This is one expected change in the features of the crisis. Another is that it is losing its identity as the 'Middle East' crisis, i.e. a regional crisis confined to a specific area. The change in the balance of force between the direct protagonists since the October war has induced the international parties concerned with the crisis to search for a new strategy. The radius of the crisis has extended to affect the non-aligned regime of Makarios in Cyprus, and the freedom of navigation in Bab el Mendeb, south of the Red Sea. The international

struggle around Somalia, Eritrea and Ethiopia has been
stepped up, not to mention the even more intense struggle in
the southern Arabian peninsula. The state of crisis spread to
the Gulf after the introduction of the oil weapon. The scope of
the conflict did not extend in the geographical sense alone, but
also in the sense that the Middle East crisis has become a link
— albeit the most explosive one — in a chain of crisis situations
of a more specific character — such as the energy crisis, the
monetary crisis, the problem of inflation, the problem of
strategic raw materials and the relationship of their prices to
those of finished products. These crises acquire geographical
features only in so far as specific points on the globe can inflame
or attenuate them.

The Middle East crisis is losing its specific character by
becoming a detonator for a network of crises of a broader scope.
Herein might lie the key to a solution, for the settlement might
be determined by the tacit agreement of various parties to
defuse the detonator. If this happens the settlement will put an
end to the Middle East crisis from the formal point of view, but
it will not put an end to the complex intermesh of crisis
situations, of a 'cybernetical' model with 'feedback' processes,
of which the Arab-Israeli conflict is one key link.

In any talk of a settlement, the Arab mind and consciousness
rebel against the idea that the only conceivable outcome of the
settlement would be compliance to Israel's strategy and
capitulation to the Zionist design.

But does a settlement with Israel necessarily signify ceding a
right? The principle of a settlement is 'neutral', in social terms.
Rejection of the principle need not be revolutionary; accepting
it does not imply a reactionary stand. The principle is
acceptable both from a revolutionary, progressive point of view
and from a reactionary, imperialist point of view. The most
important thing is the conditions of the settlement, and the
social forces it will benefit.

For example: the acceptance of a partial solution by any
Arab state at the expense of an overall settlement is typical of a
right-wing approach to the solution and would be detrimental
to the Arab cause as a whole. The fact that there are many Arab
states with different stands and interests should not be an
excuse to give in on the idea that the 'whole' has priority over
the 'part'. Otherwise we would be capitulating to the enemy

interest in dividing the Arab front, weakening all Arabs. On the other hand, this does not mean that we should reject *a priori* all partial solutions — provided that all Arabs concerned should participate.

This brings us to a particularly sensitive point: to what extent do 'partial' steps towards the settlement serve or harm a 'total' settlement? To what extent are these 'partial' steps determined by the 'vertical' contradiction with the enemy or by any other contradictions which have come to the fore? This is not the only ambiguity at this juncture. For different reasons various parties, including elements of a progressive character, do not oppose the conflict's losing its previous polarisation. The left cannot object in principle to a lessening of tensions. But certain progressive solutions liable to facilitate the settlement may be welcomed by imperialism and enlightened right-wing forces. Forces of an imperialist nature would not hesitate to make use of the Arab left and the Israeli left to facilitate a settlement on condition that the right be the main beneficiary. Incidentally, forces attributed to the left in Israel have played dubious roles at different times. A certain Israeli 'left' played a role in convincing the socialist countries that Israel would be an oasis of democracy in the Middle East. This 'left' counted on the links formed during World War Two between various groupings which were exposed to Nazi persecution in Europe, within what was known as the Zionist left and between the democratic and left movements in general. Of course this does not apply to all the left in Israel.

In fact, the settlement will acquire a progressive or reactionary, left or right, character according to the balance of power between the reactionary and progressive forces within the conflicting parties: only struggle will determine the outcome. The social content of the solution of the 'vertical' contradiction depends upon the relative weight of the forces within the region which struggle according to the 'horizontal' contradictions.

In the light of all this, what does a settlement mean in practice? It means that all parties to the dispute accept that averting war, and guaranteeing this through contractual peace agreements, is the lesser evil. It means that all parties have accepted that some sort of commensurability between them has developed. It is true of course that this alone is not a sufficient basis for contractual agreements to dissipate tension, as was proved throughout the Cold War period between the two world systems. A stable settlement would also require a mutual recognition of rights.

This means the agreement of all parties to 'freeze' the vertical contradictions between them. This does not imply the elimination of various other manifestations of conflict in the region, as conflict in general cannot be frozen.

Now the legal basis for converting the common ground into mutual recognition of rights is, in the view of the international community, the implementation of UN Security Council Resolution 242 (22 November 1967). The Security Council resolutions which were passed right after the October war demanded that Resolution 242 should be put into immediate effect. They called for a conference under the auspices of the UN in Geneva, with the participation of the US and USSR alongside the principals in the dispute, to achieve the settlement. The insistence on immediate action, after the resolution had been shelved for six years, reflects an international awareness that the threat posed by the crisis went beyond the region. It was also recognised that the October war had brought about a certain parity between the protagonists, and that in the new conditions peace talks could lead to positive results.

But Resolution 242 does not cover all aspects of the dispute nor the new developments which have arisen since the resolution was passed — specifically, the growing prominence of the Palestinian issue. The wording of the resolution contains certain ambiguities which have to be cleared up before a settlement can be reached.

For example, in their reading of the clause on 'secure and recognised borders', many have tended to oppose the notions of 'security' and that of 'sovereignty', as though the problem of Israel were one of 'security' and not of 'sovereignty', and the problem of the Arab countries subjected to occupation were one of 'sovereignty' only and not of 'security'. This is wrong both theoretically and practically. It is wrong theoretically because the sovereignty of a state is the 'form' by which its security is guaranteed. It is wrong in practice because in the course of the last quarter-century it was the security of the Arab states and not Israel's which was physically violated and Israel cannot claim the attributes of a sovereign state as long as it has no borders and refuses to declare them.

The two concepts are complementary and not contradictory. To set one off against the other would reduce the restoration of the Arab states' sovereighty to a formal concession — a cypher which, shackling this sovereignty with the constraints of Israeli security, may seem irreproachable in theory but in fact deprives it of its real significance. It would turn Israel's security into an aim whose pursuit would not be limited to its own territory but would extend to restrict the sovereignty of others.

Israel may maintain that on 4 June 1967 she had no secure and recognised borders but only armistice lines, whose vulnerability was proved by the very fact of the June war. The Arabs were justified in replying that to accept a modification of these lines would be an infringement of the Preamble to Resolution 242, which specifies that it is inadmissible to acquire territories by force. Assuming that it was justified not to identify 'secure and recognised borders' with the armistice lines of 4 June 1967, the argument cuts both ways: the state of Israel, recognised by the UN, is that of the Partition Plan of 1947, with a much lesser area than that which Israel already occupied on 4 June 1967. Moreover, what guarantees do the Arabs have that if, under the constraints of a *de facto* occupation, they accepted the principle of 'rectifications', even 'minor' ones, this acceptance would not subsequently be used against them to achieve much more substantial border changes.

For supposing that to obtain 'secure and recognised borders' two phases were necessary: first, the evacuation of occupied territories and second, final changes in the demarcation lines. Then Israel's obstinate refusal to evacuate them over the last six years and her determination to actually settle them is unlikely to generate the kind of confidence that could transform these two phases into a logical rather than a chronological sequence.

To reach agreement on 'secure and recognised borders' the following must be understood:

(1) The concept of security cannot be made to mean the security of a single state to the detriment of the neighbouring states. This is contrary not only to the UN Charter but also to the present trend towards international detente. (*Lebensraum* was discredited with Hitler.)

(2) To guarantee the security of the state through buffer zones no longer makes sense, especially in the missile age.[1] It is enough to prove only once that this system is less than invulnerable for it to lose its credibility.

(3) The interrelation between sovereignty and security for a single state is only assured by the establishment of 'interrelations' binding together the sovereignty and the security of all the states involved in the conflict. In other words, it is advisable not only to guarantee the security and sovereignty of each state by negative measures (such as demilitarised zones and the presence of the 'blue berets') but to turn the striving towards peace into an irreversible process through positive incentives also (such as industrialised belts in the regions between the belligerents).

NOTE

1. Before the October war, Israel was able to run the risk of maintaining a relatively weak garrison on the Bar-Lev line, protected as it was by its aerial superiority and reputation of invincibility. The war, having destroyed the myth of invincibility once the SAM missiles had neutralised Israel's aerial superiority, has faced Israel with the following choice: either to maintain — in the face of Egyptian defence concentration, favoured by short supply lines on the African bank — a corresponding permanent concentration on the Asian side, with the disadvantage of long supply lines across Sinai, an intolerable burden on the Israeli economy; or to withdraw.

9. The Coming War

While the new factor of 'commensurability' between the principals to the dispute which was generated by the October war could be a turning point towards peace, the delicate equilibrium produced by this event could well touch off the worst war yet in the Middle East.

Israel's absolute superiority in the past invested the situation with a degree of stability, albeit an odious one built on the spoliation of Arab rights. Another facet of this 'stability' was the Arabs' seeming inability to repel Israeli aggression, even though their loss of face acted as a constant stimulus to restitute their rights and break the *status quo*. This relative stability known as the no-war, no-peace situation, has been described by Heikal as a state of immobility in distinction to the no-victory, no-defeat situation which arose after the October war and which he described as a state of motion. This state of motion was a sudden mutation arising from the outcome of the war, in which the Arabs were no longer the vanquished and Israelis no longer the victors. The absolute superiority of Israel and the inability of the Arabs to repel Israeli aggression, which were reasons for some form of stability in the past, no longer held in the new situation. Various elements resisting a return to the no-war, no-peace situation emerged, generating a momentum which could move the crisis towards a settlement. However, unless momentum is maintained in this direction, there is no alternative in the state of motion except a swing in the opposite direction, towards a fifth war.

The general law which has governed the conflict since its inception has gradually undermined its relative stability. The definition of this law as a confrontation between Israeli quality and Arab quantity where neither side could exhaust the other could engender endless strife between them. But this definition is more an abstract concept than an expression of the real historical process: the post-1967 situation was less stable than the pre-1967 situation and the post-1973 situation is less stable than the one which held before 1973. The conflict is either moving towards a solution or towards its most dramatic explosion to date.

If it is true that elements of instability are inherent in the very nature of the conflict, it is also true that this state of instability is stretching over a wider area, i.e. the intensification of the conflict is spreading geographically and in the range of issues it embraces. It is becoming the focal point of an intricate mesh of crisis situations, without any ready solution, making a new war far from unlikely.

The Arms Race in the Middle East

The dangers have been heightened by the flood of arms pouring into the region. In the year following the October war alone $13.5 billion worth of arms made their way to the Middle East, $8.5 billion of these in the form of American arms to Israel, Iran and Saudia Arabia $4 billion (this according to western sources) in the form of Soviet arms to Syria and Egypt.

The flow of arms since the October war is significant in that it has not been confined to the countries in confrontation but has spread to cover many others, notably the oil-producing states. An even more significant development is that the quantity of arms purchased by the oil-producers is greater than that of the front-line countries. Iran's defence budget, which did not even rank among the 31 highest in the world in 1966, is today among the 15 highest in the world.

Not only have arms deals attained spectacular figures, but clients now insist on the most sophisticated weapons on the market. Such an inflow of arms, to a region festering with reasons for conflict, is making the arms producers themselves apprehensive. Some of them have put forward arguments in favour of halting the flow. One main argument is that the inflow is bound to intensify the reasons of conflict, adversely affecting their own interests. Middle East wars have proved that the surprise element is all-important. As this element depends largely on the relative superiority of the equipment used by one side or another, supplying the belligerents with ultra-sophisticated weapons encourages them to resolve the conflict by war. The range of air and sea craft now being stocked by the Middle East clients extends beyond the geographical boundaries of the region, raising the fears and suspicions of peripheral countries. India, for example, is justifiably apprehensive of Iran's rapidly escalating arms purchases.

Israel has always ensured that its military arsenal remains superior both quantitatively and qualitatively, to the combined arsenals of Arab 'confrontation countries'. In the past these were confined to Egypt, Syria and Jordan and any military assistance forthcoming from the other Arab countries was more symbolic than real. Today Saudi Arabia, Kuwait, Libya and Algeria are stockpiling highly sophisticated arms. Nor can Israel ignore Sudan, Somalia and the two Yemens after military operations during the October war extended to Bab el Mendeb. So far, the category of arms flowing into the Middle East has been within the limits of conventional weaponry — albeit the most sophisticated available — and strategic and nuclear arms were excluded from the arms race in the region. Today the situation may have changed. India has exploded its first nuclear device. This was a signal that other countries not confined to the industrially developed group of nations, or to China, could enter the nuclear club. These countries probably do not include Third World countries in the traditional sense but in the new meaning of the Third World new-rich (e.g. Iran).

Then there is Israel President Ephraim Katzir's somewhat ambiguous but chilling threat that 'Israel has the means to produce a nuclear device'. Though not conclusive proof that Israel has gone nuclear, it nevertheless indicates that this eventuality can no longer be dismissed.

However relevant these arguments may be, counter-arguments are being used to justify the difficulties in reaching any agreement to freeze arms deliveries to the region, or even in thinking that arms sales could be regulated. For example, which countries should be submitted to an embargo and which should not? The French Mirages deal to Libya raised a storm in the French National Assembly when it turned out that the proviso prohibiting Libya from using the Mirages in any war against Israel had not been respected. The same thing could happen in other Arab countries. Further, can western governments refrain from selling arms to the oil-producing countries? They could argue the validity of leaving the arms to fl w free on the grounds that binding it in any way would be seen as neo-colonialist pressure. The more telling issue is whether they can afford to prevent their arms manufacturers from concluding billion-dollar deals at a time when they are suffering grave deficits in their balance of trade, and the arms market offers an attractive way out. And, even if an embargo were imposed, can these governments prevent the Shah of Iran or Arab oil billionaires from buying up stocks and shares in arms-producing firms? The Shah has already bought 25 per cent of Krupp, while an Arab group has bought 14 per cent of Daimler-Benz, thus acquiring a say in the policy of these companies. Furthermore, conditions are now more favourable than ever before for the Arabs to set up local arms industries.

Strategic study institutes have done serious work in studying the problems of parity, both quantitative and qualitative, between the USSR and the US, on the nuclear and strategic levels, i.e. in an equation with only two parties and a limited range of arms. But this equation becomes much more intricate when the subject of study is conventional non-nuclear arms with a much wider range of diversification and when the parties are much more numerous, as is the case in the question of European security. The issue becomes even more complicated in the case of the Middle East where, unlike the 'static' equilibrium in Europe, the situation is not only volatile but quickly changing, because of the sudden increase in wealth and ability to purchase arms.

Will Israel Go to War Again?

What could lead Israel to embark on a new war? It is unlikely to be a desire to add more land to that occupied in the 1967 war, the 'ideal natural borders' guaranteeing its security without need for a settlement: the Suez Canal to the south, the Jordan river to the east and the Golan Heights to the north. The only chink in the armour is south Lebanon, which Israel considers a springboard for *fedayeen* raids into its territory.

There are valid reasons, however, why Israel might opt for war, which can be summarised as follows:

(1) To correct the impression left by the October war, and to prove that it was a transient phenomenon due to 'negligence'. If Israel is ever to admit that the October war has opened the way to a settlement, it must be on the basis of its own view of the real balance of power in the region. The settlement must be concluded along lines that would protect it from the hazards of peace.

(2) To disprove that the post-October war phenomena detrimental to Israel are irreversible and to resist the growing Palestinian problem, which could be the beginning of the end of the whole Zionist enterprise.

(3) To set its own house in order. It was thought that the Israeli establishment could weather the storm of dissent and doubt which assailed the country in the weeks following the October war but, far from being checked, the storm has continued to grow. Signs of decay began to appear: symptomatic of the deteriorating economic situation, the Israeli pound plunged by 40 per cent. Israel's image abroad was also shaken: immigration fell, tourism slackened. It is understandable that in such an atmosphere the hawks should regain a certain ascendancy and that the 'Massada complex' should grip wide sections of the Israeli public. The prophets of doom added their voice to the war cries which were being raised once more: there was no alternative but to go to war again, even in a suicidal war.

But even if Israel manages to score a sweeping victory in a coming war, has its vision of peace become a mirage that can neither be achieved by war nor by abstaining from war?

The coming war will be unlike the previous ones. The October war emphasised the importance of the missile, proving that its use in air defence could neutralise Israel's air superiority. It also proved that the infantry missile can be a tremendously effective anti-tank weapon. It is the weapon of the future in conventional warfare, cheap in comparison with other modern sophisticated arms.[1] In any coming war, it will not only be the Arab interior that will be exposed to widespread destruction. With the extension of the area exposed to reciprocal destruction, including large towns on either side, there is no guarantee that Israel will not escalate the war into a nuclear one. In such an eventuality, to quote Sadat: 'Israel might have the bomb. But if Israel introduces nuclear weapons into the region we shall not stand idly by.'

Israel can ill afford an acceleration in the tempo of military confrontations. Each new war is more damaging than the one before. The October war has proved that wars in which Arabs alone bear the full brunt are a thing of the past. For Israel, the most important factor is to guarantee unreserved American support. Yet, in the event that Israel decides to launch a new war, what guarantee is there that American and Israeli interests will coincide? Israel gives top priority to imposing its own conditions as a basis for a settlement. The US, on the other hand, is torn between two conflicting considerations: first, to stand beside Israel in finding a solution to the Middle East crisis which Israel would accept and, second, the implications of the energy crisis and Arab oil as a key to various problems besetting the western world today. Should American decision-makers find themselves pulled in two opposite directions, which issue will get priority: the Middle East crisis or the energy problem? If the Arabs decide to impose a complete oil embargo, or to blow up the wells, would the Americans decide to occupy the wells? Or will they avoid such a development by dissuading Israel from launching a war?

In face of this dilemma, Israel has three options:

(1) To attenuate its conflict of interests with the United States by choosing the moment when Israeli leverage on the US is maximal and US leverage on Israel minimal. These conditions are ideally fulfilled in the period preceding American presidential elections in 1976. All candidates will be competing for the Jewish vote and no American decision-making body would dare oppose aid to Israel, either military or political.

(2) To make Israel's interest in solving the Middle East crisis on its own conditions compatible with the United States' interest in solving the energy crisis. This could be achieved by encouraging the trend, already expressed by Ford and Kissinger, to use force against the oil-producing countries. Israel could be the instrument in this use of force, the American stick against the Arabs. The United States has never excluded the possibility of Israeli participation in such a showdown. Before the American aircraft carrier visited the Arabian Gulf late in November 1974, Schlesinger had threatened to use various means of pressure against Iran and unco-operative Arab countries, amongst which was to halt arms shipments to these countries, to send a fleet of sixty warships to the Gulf and to speed up re-arming Israel. Schlesinger pointed out that Israel's military arsenal since the October war has been better stocked than ever before. According to this pattern, a fifth war will be a repeat performance of the second Arab-Israeli war, with the US replacing Britain and France. This time the pretext would be to protect the source of energy; in 1956, it was to

oppose nationalisation of the Suez Canal. In both cases, it is the protection of western interests and 'civilisation' from the Arab 'barbarians'. These arguments, now heard in Israel, are reminiscent of those used by Eden and Mollet in 1956. The advantage of this second option for Israel is that, unlike the first, it does not link the launching of a war to a given date but leaves it very flexible. Israel can choose a moment when the western world in general is most affected by the energy crisis, and with the support of the world Zionist movement, could convince the West that, though it might be challenging international legality, it is only undertaking an unavoidable preventive measure to protect the values of western civilisation.

Arab reactions could go so far as to blow up the wells; any American intervention, even if it wears an Israeli glove, is bound to provoke reactions from the socialist countries. Therefore the ideal moment for Israel would be when it can convince the United States that it has no choice but to either expose détente to danger or the economies of the West to a fatal collapse. Saving one's own skin obviously has priority over avoiding provoking the other party.

(3) To coincide the next war with the presidential elections and to combine with the presidential campaign promoting the use of force against Arab oil producers, which would harmonise with the anti-détente forces in the United States, led by Senator Jackson.

These are three options open to Israel. Meanwhile, a fourth option can be promoted by the United States, which could occupy some key oil installations, Dahran for example, simultaneously calling for Israeli withdrawal from occupied Arab territories. In this way it will have imposed its control over the flow and price of Arab oil, it will have neutralised Europe and will have attenuated Arab reactions to its operation by effecting the Israeli withdrawal. Meanwhile, Israel's security will in no way be threatened as the withdrawal will come at a time when US hegemony over the region will be at its strongest.

For the Arabs, a fifth war would be a repeat performance not of the second Arab-Israeli war, but, rather, a second edition of the fourth: to complete what the October war failed to achieve. Though it broke the stalemate and created a movement towards a solution of the crisis, the war of its own did not generate enough momentum to achieve it. Should the Arabs opt for war they would have many problems. Many Arab states do not want this war to serve the cause of the Arab rejectionists, who are totally opposed to any settlement with Israel. However, if certain Arab countries made a partial settlement with Israel which other Arab states saw as threatening the chances of total settlement, the latter would not be inhibited by the support of the rejectionists in a further war. Any partial agreement carries within it two opposite possibilities: either to bring a total settlement within reach or to push it completely out of sight. Israel will not give up trying to use any partial agreement to isolate certain Arab parties in the hope of knocking one party after another out of the game. Israel's original intention in signing any partial agreement could be to induce the parties outside the agreement to react to it in a manner that would serve Israel's own interest in waging a war. To have a war launched without assuming the responsibility for such an action would suit Israel very well.

In any event the Arabs must prepare for the eventuality of war, using all the weapons at their disposal, if only to deter Israel, to increase their bargaining power or even to use it as an additional leverage along with the other weapons they possess. But even while preparing for war, the Arab's best chances for avoiding a fifth war lie in the effective use of these other weapons.

NOTE

1. Sixteen launching pads and 80 missiles cost no more than one modern tank. Military strategists say that infantry carrying light missiles will regain great importance in future wars.

10. Arab Weapons

Since the October war the Arabs have possessed new weapons hitherto unheard of in the political idiom: 'Arab oil', 'Arab capital', and the ability to cause violent upheavals in world monetary markets. How potent are these weapons?

With much fanfare, the western press has pointed out that oil-producing countries' revenue in the oil output from their territories rose from $1 per barrel in 1970 to £1.99 just before the October war, jumped to $3.44 by the end of 1973 and reached $10 by the end of 1974: with the result that the coffers of the thirteen OPEC countries took in $112 billion in just one year. As this amount exceeds their spending capacity, these countries accumulated a payments surplus of $60 billion — that is, the surplus increased at the rate of $164 million a day, or $6.8 million an hour. This was the swiftest transfer of money in history and the West panicked. Influential news media tried to lay the blame for the economic disturbances in the western world on the October war and the increase in oil prices which followed, prophesying imminent disaster and advancing evidence that the capitalist countries were in the throes of their severest recession since the Great Depression of the Thirties.

Before going to the core of the problem we should warn against certain distortions in this defamatory campaign against the OPEC countries. In the logic of world monopolies and multinational companies, not only is price-raising not a crime, but is considered the legitimate means by which to maximise profits. It would seem, therefore that this practice is condemned only when used by countries of the non-developed world. Neither is it justified to claim that the OPEC countries constitute a cartel which imposes prices in defiance of the law of supply and demand and which took advantage of the launching of the October war to catch the consumer by surprise, forcing him either to buy at 'unfair' prices or to succumb to the 'squeeze'.

OPEC performs a function closer to that of workers' unions than that of capitalist monopolies. Describing it as a 'cartel' is a misleading description put out by imperialist propaganda.

These arguments are contradictory because both practices — price-raising and seizing opportunities — are basic components of the system followed by western monopolies.

Moreover, the demand for oil did not diminish dramatically when prices were raised. Even if it did diminish slightly this only showed that consumers had been wasting energy because of its extremely low price. It was used, for instance, to over-illuminate highways in Europe and to provide gasoline for the excessively powerful cars in America. What do the oil consumers consider a 'fair' price? Is it the cost of extraction? Oil companies claim that this fluctuates between a maximum $2.5 per bbl in the United States and a minimum of 12 cents per bbl in Saudi Arabia. This low cost of extraction in the Arab countries obviously reflects intense exploitation of the Arab worker, as there is no qualitative difference in the conditions of extraction or in the cost of equipment used. If the cost of extraction is the criterion, then how do the oil companies justify their exorbitant profits which attained $5.3 billion for the five majors alone in the year preceding the October war and leaped to $8.2 billion in the year immediately following the war?

It cannot be denied that the price of oil must have some market relationship to the price of alternative sources of energy. These are many: shale-oil, deep-sea oil and oil from remote regions like Alaska which is costly to obtain, requiring as it does a technology of its own. In addition, other sources of energy not derived from oil, like nuclear energy (possibly also solar energy before the end of this century) are being studied. If the cost of what corresponds to 1 bbl of oil from an alternate source of energy is, say $10, then it is absurd that the cost of a bbl of oil should remain at the level of $2. This cannot be considered 'fair' according to the very logic of supply and demand. It should be remembered that all forecasts made by western industrialised countries in the late fifties predicted that nuclear energy would become competitive around 1975. This date was not fixed arbitrarily, nor simply to allow a margin for research in this domain but because the industrialised countries were aware that the ever-increasing consumption of energy would use up proven global oil reserves soon after the turn of the century.

Arab and Irani oil constitute 70 per cent of proven commercial oil reserves. The low price of oil (which for a long time remained lower than its 'normal' competitive market price) led to a slackening in the quest for alternate sources of energy, which was shelved through the sixties. After the October war, western industrialised countries were suddenly confronted with an abrupt increase in oil prices. This increase corrected an unnatural situation. As consuming countries had hoped that this unnatural situation would continue indefinitely they did not take the necessary precautions at the right moment. This is the explanation for the 'energy crisis'.

It is not due to a lack of adequate sources of energy to meet humanity's increasing needs. It is only a temporary bottleneck, caused by neglect in the search for alternative sources of energy, the fact that not enough funds were allocated for the necessary research, in the hope that cheap oil could continue to be used.

More fallacies need to be cleared up. It is not true that all industrial countries opposed the increase in oil prices. Nor is it true that this increase is wholly, or essentially, responsible for the economic crisis which the West is exposed to today.

The United States has often said that the 'optimum price' of a bbl of oil is $7 (the price fixed at the OPEC meeting in Tehran in December 1973) and not the $2 at which it stood before the 1973 war. In other words, the US did not oppose a 350 per cent increase in the price of oil, which would, according to French experts, realise an increase of $15 billion in America's surplus and $31 billion in the Arabs' surplus between 1974 and 1980. This will be at the expense of Europe ($22 billion), Latin America ($11.5 billion), South-east Asia ($10 billion) and Japan ($9.6 billion).* It is also the ideal price to consolidate the position of American oil companies in the international oil industry, to strike a decisive blow at the aspirations of Europe and Japan to compete with the USA in world markets and to stimulate scientific research for alternative sources of energy inside the US by underlining their competitive aspects (American oil companies have actually

---

*On the assumption that prices remain stable.

begun to invest part of their huge surpluses in scientific research in this domain). It also reveals America's design to absorb the Arab world as a basis for regaining its global hegemony, and to make Arab oil-producing countries a Trojan Horse inside the Third World. However, in 1974 the price of a bbl of oil jumped from the optimum $7 to $10. Not only did this price no longer suit their interests, but the Americans were alarmed that the situation might 'get out of hand'. And so the American press loudly condemned the Arab oil-producing countries and President Ford and Dr Kissinger hinted at possible armed intervention to put an end to the 'chaos' in the world economy for which the Middle East oil skeikhs were held entirely responsible.

How true is it in fact that the increase in oil prices is responsible for this 'chaos' in the world economy and for inflation in the West? Although this does not purport to be a detailed study of the issue, it is perhaps worth mentioning here that western experts have calculated the contribution of the oil price rise to the rate of inflation at no more than 1 or 2 per cent. Even if we avoid using arguments of figures and percentages which leave room for different interpretations, the very concrete fact is that the phenomenon of inflation preceded the sudden rise in oil prices by quite some time. The first signs of the economic crisis began to appear in the US ten years ago.

After its famous crisis in 1929, and especially since World War Two, the world capitalist economy has undergone a basic change. The phenomenon of severe cyclic crises which used to plague the economy at the rate of approximately one crisis every ten years had disappeared. After World War Two it seemed that capitalism had succeeded in producing the permanently affluent society.

But the very same reasons which led to the disappearance of the cyclic crises led to the state of stagnation in the western economy some years ago and also explain why the current crisis has attained such grave dimensions. The world capitalist system regained a large measure of vitality in the two post-war decades (1945-65) thanks to the convergence of three factors: the scientific and technological revolution; new forms of relationships with the Third World (a source of cheap energy and raw materials for the West); and the development of 'state capitalism'. Thanks to the scientific and technological revolution, the capitalist system developed new methods to consolidate its hegemony and extended its sphere of activities to the field of consumption. It developed new branches of production, namely electronics and petro-chemicals. It also liquidated all pre-capitalist forms of production, especially in the domain of agriculture.

After most of the Third World countries achieved their political independence, the new system of neo-colonialism was devised to replace traditional colonial rule. The United States in particular played a prominent role in filling the 'void' created by the collapse of European colonialism. The basis of the new relations was the looting of sources of energy and raw materials in the developing countries at 'unfair' prices out of all proportion to the rising prices of finished products in developed countries.

And, finally, world capitalism profited from the lessons which John Maynard Keynes drew from the crisis of 1929. Keynes was the first non-Marxist economist who realised the role which the modern state could play in minimising economic upheavals by the use of various economic regulators. His ideas were the blueprint for Roosevelt's New Deal after the Depression of 1929. His theories encouraged the development of strong links between giant corporations and the state, which led to state capitalism.

All these developments gave the impression that cyclic economic crises had disappeared for ever. This impression was dispelled when Europe and Japan started to regain relative economic independence in the sixties and when competition between developed capitalist countries was stepped up. The United States's share in the total production of the West fell from 70 per cent in 1950 to 57 per cent in 1965 to 49 per cent in 1973. Beginning in 1973, the rate of growth of the American economy fell to nil. Self-financing became more and more difficult and the only way to stimulate it was by resorting to inflation and by recycling petrodollars to bolster American industry. To attenuate its own crisis, the US exported inflation to the world capitalist world through Eurodollars. As a result, the American balance of trade was upset and the crisis began to take concrete shape. Each western country tried separately to solve its own problem of inflation. Deficits in the balance of payments began to appear in industrial countries. It was in this atmosphere of incipient crisis that the October war broke out. The ensuing rise in oil prices led to an increase in prices of finished goods, making the consumer carry the burden of inflation. This accelerated inflation.

Due to the reluctance of welfare societies to impose austerity measures in the cause of increasing exports, many western countries failed to bridge the gap in their balance of trade. Production was cut, restrictions were imposed on loans and unemployment soared, leading to the now familiar symptoms of recession: the collapse of small firms to the advantage of bigger ones, excessive build-up of stocks and the paralysis of the key industries which two decades earlier had invigorated the economy. It is clear therefore that the increase in the price of oil did not cause inflation, but only made it more blatant.

The Effects of the Oil Revolution

There are two aspects to the sudden rise in Arab oil prices. The first is the revolutionary, progressive aspect. This applies in the sense that this is a first step for the Third World countries which produce strategic raw materials in regaining the right to adjust the prices of what they produce and for the prices of raw materials to become compatible with those of finished products. The example set by the OPEC countries will not be confined to oil alone, but is a model for Third World countries producing other raw materials. This development is significant after the setback in Chile when the CIA succeeded in overthrowing Allende, because Chile was pressing for a similar improvement in the price of copper just before the October war.

It has been contended that the battle of OPEC was a unique case because the most important oil reserves were concentrated in one area; and the countries of the region acted because of the Middle East crisis and the October war. The oil-producing countries could for the first time reduce their oil output and impose embargoes on certain countries because they had achieved surplus wealth in the preceding period which enabled them to take these steps without serious threat to their economy. As a matter of fact, it was in their interest to limit production because of the monetary crisis. Arab oil wealth was more secure and more permanent in the ground than it was exposed to currency fluctuations. On the other hand, consuming countries had not taken the necessary precautions against the sudden price increase as they did not expect the

Arabs to wage the October war, nor that they would use the oil weapon in this war. They were taken unawares at a time when they were gripped by inflation.

Whatever can be said about the unique situation in which oil prices were raised, and although it is unlikely that so many factors would again unite to produce the same results, the fact remains that this increase marked the beginning of a process. Sooner or later it will go beyond oil. In this sense the Arabs' battle to build wealth from oil can be considered revolutionary. Arab wealth in this meaning is not the antithesis of Arab revolution. Limiting the flow of oil, imposing an embargo and raising oil prices were weapons in the Arab liberation struggle not only against Zionist and Israeli expansionism, but also against the very foundations of contemporary world imperialism and of the capitalist world economy — in other words, it became a weapon in the struggle for liberation in its widest meaning.

But this is only one side of the coin. The other is that the adjustment in oil prices was not unrelated to the manipulations of global finance and imperialism, and specifically American determination to strengthen its world competitive position and to consolidate its own status as the unchallenged superpower of the western world. It should be remembered in this connection that Kissinger said to *Newsweek's* Arnaud de Borchgrave six months before the October war that a shock in the Middle East could have salutary effects.

In that sense the accumulation of Arab wealth is in opposition to Arab revolution. There is a danger that the displacement of billions of dollars from the consuming to the oil-producing countries will be more nominal than real. It is essential that Arab oil and Arab wealth should retain their attributes as Arab weapons in the battle for the Middle East. It is not enough that the Arabs should possess enormous bank deposits in the West, or that they should indulge in speculation, property or buy shares in giant corporations like IBM, Krupp, Mercedes and others. All this is simply helping these companies ride out the storm of recession. In other words, Arab wealth is here deployed to bolster Europe's shaky economy instead of achieving tangible benefits for the Arab peoples.

More important, the Arabs should not let their surpluses lie idle to be seized by the West to solve its own crisis at the expense of legitimate Arab rights. Arabs must be masters of their own capital. The fate of petrodollars should not be determined outside the Arab world. When the Arabs let their surpluses lie dormant, they allow others to impose the burden of inflation upon them and deprive them of the ability to follow the world-side increase in prices which extends to food products and threatens the poor countries. In the final analysis it means that the new Arab wealth will only enrich strata or individuals and will not contribute to the development of the Arab peoples. Unless it is used to promote Arab development Arab wealth will become increasingly divorced from the land that produced it until the oil dries up.

The Arab nation should have a decisive say in how these assets are to be used. It is hard to see how the Arab oil-producing countries, some of which are limited in area and population, can absorb these enormous surpluses by investing them in separate internal projects. This does not mean that these surpluses should be left to the oil-consuming countries. Part of these surpluses must be allocated to purchase the technology the Arabs need, provided this serves Arab development. This can only be conceived within a strategy of Arab integration and according to joint ventures decided by a long-term pan-Arab plan.

According to this plan, the Arabs would regain complete control over all sources of their wealth. To achieve this aim they should not fear nationalisation. This does not necessarily imply 'isolationism', or departing from the principle of international co-operation and exchange. Arab integration is not only required to avoid competitive projects but also to extend the Arab market and to increase demand. This not only entails investment in refineries, petrochemical industries or steel, aluminium and other heavy industry projects; but also in desalination of sea-water to meet Arab food requirements, in developing fishing industries in the Gulf, the Red Sea and the Mediterranean, or in developing agriculture in the virgin regions of Sudan, Somalia or even in the Fertile Crescent. It also entails setting up basic infrastructures like extensive networks of roads, railways and airways betweens the Arab countries, as well as establishing an Arab commercial fleet, in order to transform Arab integration into a living reality.

But a *solution* to the Middle East crisis can only be found

in a just solution to the original cause of the conflict: the
Palestinian problem.

11. The Palestinian Problem

Arab delegates, including the Palestinians, used to spurn our attempts to speak to them. Now it would appear that they have regained confidence in themselves, for they make no secret of their desire to talk to us.' These are the words of Naphtalie Feder, National Secretary of the 'Zionist Socialist' Mapam party of Israel, in an interview during the World Peace council meeting in Prague early in 1975 with the French weekly *Le Nouvel Observateur*. According to the interview, it was Feder who was reluctant to talk with the PLO respresentative at the meeting. 'What could he add to what I have already heard Yasser Arafat say on the rostrum of the United Nations? Egypt and Syria want to regain the territories they lost in 1967. That is a clear and definite aim. But what does the PLO want? Its declared objective is the destruction of the state of Israel. Can this be a basis for negotiation?' The Palestinian question still represents the most intricate problem in the Middle East crisis.

Israel does not admit to the existence of a problem, or at least of the problem as defined by the Arab side or by ever widening circles of international public opinion. Very few Zionists, like Nahum Goldman, see the need to deal with the PLO. Even if occasional Israeli statements indicate some sort of recognition of a 'Palestinian reality', these statements always maintain that it should not acquire an existence independent from Jordan. This is the stand of the ruling Ma'arech Party in Israel. The Mapam's stand, as stated by Feder, is that a prerequisite for any Israeli negotiation with a party representing Palestine is that party's recognition of Israel and the cessation of 'terrorism'.

What is most startling in Feder's statement is his allegation that a responsible representative of the PLO tried to open a discussion with a responsible representative of the Israeli establishment, though the PLO's declared objective is to set up a secular, democratic state in Palestine in place of the state of Israel.

Any contact between an Arab official and an Israeli official in the past, or even between ordinary citizens on either side, would have been considered an extraordinary event. After the October war, however, the whole world saw pictures of generals Gamassy and Yariv at the first disengagement talks at kilometre 101 on the Suez road. Certainly of all the Arabs the Palestinians have had the most intercourse with the Israeli authorities, if only because they have lived under Israeli occupation for many years and because both Israel and Jordan have been keen on keeping the flow of traffic over the Allenby bridge across the river Jordan open. However, Israeli authorities refuse categorically to have dealings with any Palestinian resistance organizations. They only deal with those Palestinians whom the believe have accepted the *fait accompli*, and they are relentless in their pursuit of those who will not submit to the Israeli order or even those suspected of harbouring a Palestinian resistance fighter. Israeli retaliatory measures include detention, persecution, torture, destroying homesteads and even the razing of entire villages.

For a long time the principals in the Middle East crisis clung to the rules of the Cold War period. The conflict was marked by complete polarisation and the only intercourse between the conflicting parties took place on the battlefield. The October war put an end to this pattern and created new conditions for the relationship between the Arab confrontation states and Israel, affected by the rules of détente. The Palestinian problem, however, was not included in this change. So far there is still no intercourse between Israeli authorities and the Palestinian resistance except the language of the gun. In other words, the Palestinian question is the only aspect of the crisis which is still marked by the rules of the Cold War and which has not been affected by the rules of détente.

That is why any dialogue between a representative of the PLO and an Israeli official may appear strange. It is a dialogue which Israel has always categorically refused, all the more adamantly since the PLO acquired greater stature after the October war, disproving the theory that the status it had attained before the war was due only to the fact that the PLO symbolised the will to resist after the Arab states were defeated.

Israel's logic is that while the principle of carrying on a dialogue with the neighbouring Arab states according to the rules of détente is possible — provided it realises peace on

Israel's terms or at least on terms acceptable to Israel — no dialogue is possible with the PLO which Israel considers a collection of assassins and terrorists.

Can the rules of détente be applied to all aspects of the Middle East crisis, including the Palestinian problem? Can a basis for intercourse between Israel and the PLO, as the representative of the Palestinian people, be worked out — if only because the present intercourse through the barrel of the gun could undermine the entire settlement in the Middle East? According to some western sources, a blueprint for an agreement on the Palestinian problem was fixed by Brezhnev and Ford in Vladivostock: the idea being that Moscow should convince the Palestinians to recognise Israel's right to exist while the US should convince Israel to recognise the PLO.

This would mean a switch from a state of mutual non-recognition to one of mutual recognition. A certain disparity between the case of Israel versus Palestine and the case of Israel versus the Arab states should be noted in this connection. In the case of Israel versus Palestine there is complete symmetry: either mutual non-recognition or mutual recognition. In the case of Israel versus the Arab states, on the other hand, the situation is asymmetrical in that the Arab states do not recognise Israel while Israel cannot but recognise the Arab states and strives to obtain their formal recognition.

However, the mutation in the Israeli-Palestinian relationship is fraught with seemingly insurmountable difficulties, as it would affect the very existence of both parties and their basic philosophies. Each side's claim to the land of Palestine is based on the negation of the other side's claim. The 'right' of the Jewish people to a national home in Palestine is the very essence of the Zionist design and any constraint on this 'right' would jeopardise it. Similarly, the right of the Palestinians to the land which Israel usurped is of the same absolute character. On the practical level too, many obstacles will come up.

If Israel is to recognise a Palestinian entity it would be giving up the basic Zionist premise which holds that Israel represents the 'return of a people without a land to a land without a people'. True, Israel no longer interprets this premise quite so literally, given that it can hardly pretend that Palestine was uninhabited before the Zionist colonisation. But to go on to admit that the original Arab inhabitants constituted a people and a distinct national entity would place Israel in a dilemma, affecting its own internal structure. For example, admitting the existence of a non-Jewish people inside Palestine, even outside Israel, with rights equivalent to those of the Israelis, affects the very basis of the racist hierarchy in Israel, which distinguishes between the Jews themselves (western and eastern) — not to mention the status of the Arabs as second-class citizens. How could Israel then admit rights to the Arab Palestinians outside Israel which are not given to Jews inside Israel, although Israel purports to be the 'national home' of world Jewry?

Even if the PLO were to accept Israel, it would not necessarily have renounced its objective to set up a secular, democratic state in the whole of Palestine. It might mean only that it had deferred this objective to a later stage and that its acceptance of Israel was only transitory, even if the dismantling of Israel was to be achieved by different means than those practised until now. A substantial portion of Israeli opinion firmly believes this and will go on believing it even if the PLO accepts the Mapam's demands for recognition of Israel and the renunciation of what Feder calls 'terrorism'. These sceptics have one valid argument which is that even if the PLO accepts Israel it will only be a *de facto* recognition stemming from a realistic assessment of the balance of power in the region at this juncture. But there will always be Palestinians who will continue fighting to restore their right over the whole of Palestine.

From the Israeli point of view, the PLO's participation in the settlement contains an inconsistency. The PLO, unlike all other participants at the negotiation table, does not confine its final vision of the future of Palestine to what will be finalised in the settlement. The PLO might accept the settlement, but it will only regard it as valid for an interim period. This is completely unacceptable to Israel, on the grounds that if it is to accept the Palestinians as a party to a settlement, then all parties must respect the principle of the totality of the settlement and its irrevocability.

The real difficulty is that the PLO's acceptance of Israel in fact implies that it is renouncing its bid to set up the secular state at least in the medium term. This postponement could go on indefinitely and, as such, would be ceding a fundamental principle and a basic right. Furthermore, accepting Israel would imply, from the point of view of principle, accepting Zionist rule over a portion of Palestine and repelling Zionism only in its expansionist expression, which would keep the threat of Zionism alive. From the practical point of view, this acceptance would mean relinquishing for ever *fedayeen* activities inside Israel. Opinions may differ as to the ethics of this mode of struggle, but no one can deny that it has had tremendous impact in attracting world attention to the plight of the Palestinians.

However profound the reasons for mutual non-recognition between Israel and the PLO, however, there are considerations which compel the two sides to consider how to overcome the impasse.

Forcing Israel to pull back and to deliver territories to the Palestinians for them to govern according to their independent will is a step forward towards the Palestinian objectives that cannot be disregarded.

Before the October war there were in fact two Arab stands:

The first stand took removing the consequences of the aggression of 1967 as its brief, i.e. basing the settlement on the restitution of the Arab territories occupied by Israel in the 1967 war. This stand is embodied in the Security Council Resolution 242. It is, *grosso modo,* the stand of the Arab states who lost territory in 1967. As the Palestinian problem became more acute, an additional, distinct Arab demand was added to the original terms of reference: the recognition of the national rights of the Palestinian people. This in fact meant that the Palestinian problem would find a solution in the wake of the solution of the Arab states' problem.

The second stand's brief was 'removing the consequences of the aggression of 1948', i.e. to wipe out the Zionist state as a basis for the settlement. Any settlement that did not require the destruction of the Zionist state was rejected as being a stabilisation of Israel. This was the stand adopted by the Palestinian resistance movement — the slogan of 'throwing the Jews into the sea' attributed to Shukeiry is not its only expression. It is also expressed in Fatah's objective to erecting a secular, democratic state in Palestine for Jews, Christians and Moslems in place of the racist creation of Isreal. This meant focusing Arab strategy on achieving the Palestinian objective and solving the Arab states' problem in its wake.

As long as Israel occupied the whole of Palestine and large

slices of the territories of neighbouring Arab states after the
1967 war, there was no practical criterion to prove that one
stand was more appropriate than the other as a basis for the
Arab strategy.

Things changed after the October war. By launching the war
Egypt and Syria brought the objective of removing the
consequences of the aggression of 1967 within reach. With the
first disengagement agreements both countries recovered a
portion of their occupied territories. A conference to achieve an
overall settlement was convened. Such a settlement cannot but
include the Palestinian territory occupied since the 1967 war,
and so the PLO found itself confronted by a dilemma: would it
assume national authority over every square inch of liberated
Palestinian territory or should these lands return to the
sovereignty of Jordan? Where the PLO to opt for the former, it
would be acquiescing in the existence of two entities in
Palestine, the Palestinian and the Israeli, for an indefinite
stretch of time. This contradicts the PLO's declared objective
to erect a secular state in all Palestine.

Opting for the latter, on the other hand, would imply an
admission that Palestinian territory could be administered and
submitted to the sovereignty of a third party, a denial of its
raison d'être as sole representative of the Palestinian people.
The PLO had to choose and chose to give up the logic that the
Zionist entity had to be totally uprooted before the principle of
settlement talks could be accepted. After the October war the
Palestinian National Council passed a resolution instructing
the PLO to assume responsibility over every square inch of
reclaimed Palestinian territory. The PLO could no longer
remain a disinterested party to the settlement talks. Obviously
if the talks result in a settlement the PLO is bound to realise
that its chances of pursuing *fedayeen* activities will be
drastically reduced, because any agreement will bind the Arab
signatories to deny the *fedayeen* the use of their territories.

Furthermore, the settlement talks in which the PLO is
somehow involved will include Israel, which refuses to deal with
any party that does not recognise it — not to mention a party
whose declared objective is to eliminate it.

However, Israel cannot totally disregard the PLO either,
whatever the PLO's stand might be. After all, the very logic of
a settlement is an overall agreement with the Arabs and this

can neither be visualised nor substantiated without the PLO's inclusion. Israel might try to avoid any dealings with the PLO, and reiterate that it will only undertake negotiations over Palestinian territory with King Hussein. Even if a Palestinian entity is to be accepted, Israel still insists that it should not have sovereign rights outside the Hashemite kingdom. Israel will not give up this logic unless forced to: the various pressures which could be exerted on it can be summarised as follows:

(1) Arab pressure on King Hussein to hand over the West Bank to the PLO.

(2) Pressure by the inhabitants of the West Bank to have the PLO as their sole representative.

(3) US pressure on Israel to refrain from dealing with Jordan in what concerns the West Bank.

So far the US has refused to exert this pressure. Indeed, before the Rabat summit the US exerted pressure on the Arabs to prevent them passing a resolution designating the PLO as responsible for all Palestinian land recovered from Israel. But US pressure in this direction is not without limits: the United States cannot ignore the Palestinian diaspora in the oil-producing countries as a potential fuse to blow up the oil-wells. As for Arab pressure on King Hussein, it did in fact induce him at Rabat to accept the PLO as responsible for the West Bank. His view was clearly stated: I am better placed than the PLO to regain control over the West Bank. After I achieve this the Palestinian people will be free to decide their own fate. Do not tie my hands. But, if you consider it best that the PLO should assume the responsibility of the West Bank as of now, it must assume it totally. Let us see what it can achieve.

The king took a step backwards in Rabat, but this did not prevent the Israelis from continuing to regard him as the valid spokesman for the West Bank. In fact, the king's position at Rabat was an astute reminder that he holds a trump card. Last but not least is the pressure exerted by the West Bank inhabitants themselves for the PLO to be the sole representative of the Palestinian people. What the Palestinian people impose by their struggle inside occupied territory is decisive. This struggle is gaining growing momentum and is one of the most prominent signs of the emerging Palestinian personality.

In view of this, Israel might have no alternative but to deal with some kind of Palestinian representation. In fact, it has already set the basis for a so-called Palestinian administration by holding municipal elections in the West Bank in 1972. These elections did not aim only at entrenching the Israeli occupation but also at creating the nucleus of an alternative Palestinian authority, drawing its 'legitimacy' from the occupying authorities.[1]

This scheme was not promoted by Israel alone but was also furthered by King Hussein. His project to set up the United Arab Kingdom facilitated the scheme, not because the project referred to an autonomous Palestinian province within his kingdom (there is no question of implementing the project before Israeli withdrawal) but because it was to be implemented by Palestinian leaders loyal to the king who are openly dealing with both the occupation authorities and the king across the open bridges of the Jordan river.

Israel is certain to insist that only Palestinians from within Palestine, drawing their legitimacy from their traditional loyalty to the Hashemite kingdom, can represent the Palestinians people. In fact Israel will spare no effort to find some alternate Palestinian representation to scuttle PLO representation and to undermine the very foundations of an independent Palestinian state. That is why the PLO cannot afford to leave the Palestinian seat empty — as soon as such a seat is agreed upon — in any future settlement.

The problem is that Israel is gambling on the fact that the Palestinian resistance movement is still divided betweens the official leadership and the rejectionists. The official leadership's reputation is built on their history of armed struggle against the Zionist usurper, their image as symbols of Palestinian defiance and Arab inflexibility. These leaders, notably the Fatah leadership, are generally recognised as the authorised representatives of the Palestinian people.

The PLO can no longer afford to have only a military strategy of armed struggle and *fedayeen* action against Israel. Today it requires a political strategy. Its concern is to win over wider sections of world opinion and gain further official recognition, without having to renounce certain forms of struggle condemned by international law and opinion. These political considerations will not carry the same weight for all

Palestinian fighters as long as international support does not produce any concrete results. Until these results are achieved, there will always be room for the 'rejectionist front'. Israel's description of them as out-and-out terrorists is shared by much of world opinion. They categorically refuse the idea of a settlement or of any dialogue with Israel other than through the barrel of the gun. They view any eventual PLO acceptance of a settlement as a sell-out.

Their position is bound to attract wider sections of the Palestinian resistance the more obstinately Israel refuses to deal with the PLO. In the name of condemning 'violence and terrorism', by refusing to recognise the PLO, Israel is in fact helping violence to flourish.

If the relationship between Israel and the PLO is to pass from mutual non-recognition to mutual recognition, what form can this take? One obvious form could be based on international legality, i.e. making UN resolutions the terms of reference, since terms of reference based on the outlook of the PLO or that of Israel are impossible in view of their complete irreconcilability. Applying international legality would mean applying all UN resolutions on Palestine — including the UN resolution of 29 November 1947 on the partition of Palestine into an Arab Palestinian state and Israel. If the PLO is reluctant to initiate this line, it might accept it in response to a request from the Arab states.

The PLO's acceptance of the concept of partition would not imply that it has renounced its objective to establish a secular state for Jews, Christians and Moslems in Palestine. It must be remembered that the partition resolution was not passed originally in opposition to the idea of an Arab-Jewish state in Palestine, but only because the setting up of such a state was not practical at the time. Nor is it feasible now, or in the near future, a fact that the PLO itself does not deny. By accepting the Partition Plan, the PLO would invalidate the Israeli accusation that it is a terrorist organisation, an outcast from international legality, unauthorised to speak for the Palestinians in the settlement talks. Accepting partition will also enhance the PLO's image internationally, giving further impetus to its achievements which culminated in Yasser Arafat's address to the General Assembly of the UN. Partition implies a *de facto* recognition of the existence of both an

Israeli and a Palestinian entity in Palestine, if not the final configuration of each. As establishing borders cannot be finalised outside or before the settlement talks, the vital problem at this juncture is to include the legal representatives of the Palestinian people in these talks.

Partition will also put an end to the dispute between the PLO and Jordan. The West Bank was held in trust by Jordan for as long as no definite solution to the Palestinian problem had been reached. Should an Arab Palestinian state based on UN resolutions be set up, Jordan's claim to the West Bank would no longer stand before the PLO's right to this territory. It goes without saying that any such bid on the part of the PLO would be flatly rejected by Israel on the grounds that it would deprive it of wide territories which Israel considers part and parcel of its being, beginning from the war of 1948.

Such a claim has no legal basis, for the Israel recognised by the United Nations is the Israel which the United Nations created according to the Partition Plan. All lands annexed by Israel since were seized by force. This is in direct violation of a clause in the Preamble to Resolution 242 and, what is more important, with regard to terrorists annexed before 1967, of the UN Charter.

Now even if the PLO does not 'formalise' its relationship with Israel according to the Partition Plan, the realities discussed in this chapter cannot still be dismissed. These realities do not require the PLO to give up its final objective but require it, given the current balance of power, to admit that obtaining Israeli recognition is a prerequisite for achieving its final objective in the future. Of course, recognition of Israel could mean that the PLO's objective will never be realised. However, the PLO must be aware that non-recognition of Israel exposes it to the danger of not being able to set up a Palestinian national authority over any portion of Palestinian territory. This impasse, which will become more explosive as time goes on, might satisfy certain trends within the resistance movement. But such a deteriorating situation will be resisted by numerous parties concerned with the crisis, including parties that cannot be described as hostile to the Palestinian cause.

If what has been attributed to Ford and Brezhnev in Vladivostok is true, it would mean that the two superpowers expect Israel and Palestine to establish relations inspired by those which détente has set up between the Soviet Union and the United States. Although the Soviet Union has not renounced its ultimate goal of building Communism the world over and the United States has not renounced its aim to eradicate Communism, peaceful coexistence is possible. Each system remains convinced that it can achieve its ultimate goal through peace instead of through a Cold War that can flare up into a nuclear holocaust. In the case of Israel versus Palestine, this would mean that the PLO will not be required to renounce its ultimate goal of a secular state in place of Israel and that Israel will not be required to renounce the basic Zionist premise that it embodies. Once a settlement is achieved on these grounds, each side will have to prove that it has the best assets to survive the other and to foil the other's aim by means within the norms of international legality and the international system established since the birth of détente.[2]

NOTES

1. The recent municipal elections in occupied territories in 1976 completely defeated this Israeli design. In spite of occupation, the overwhelming majority of votes went to candidates whose PLO sympathies are no secret. These elections are a major development in the whole Middle East situation.
2. A further development on the Palestinian problem was presented by the author in a paper to the 'Palestine Colloquium' which was held in Brussels (13—15 May 1976). See Appendix.

12. Post-Settlement Perspectives

Does the Arab-Israeli conflict in its historical perspective bear comparison with the Crusades? Stretching over two centuries they were a series of incursions responding to a widespread call in Christendom to regain control of the holy city of Jerusalem and the surrounding land of Palestine. Today there is a widespread belief among Moslems that the Arab and Moslem world is exposed to something similar, this time responding to a call in the Jewish world: the call of Zionism to establish a national home for world Jewry — also in the land of Palestine.

Even in the twentieth century religion has stirred deep feelings to restore a temporal existence to each of the three monotheist religions in this holy land. Perhaps the religious element was not the motivating or decisive factor in either the case of the Crusades six centuries ago or in the creation of Israel in the twentieth century. But religion definitely played an important role in inflaming volatile emotions and in convincing wide segments of public opinion of the righteousness of such undertakings regardless of the many obstacles in their way.

Though the Crusades were driven back they left behind them Christian communities which settled in the region and which today form, together with the original Christian inhabitants, a prominent element in the communal set-up of modern Lebanon.

Will Israel evolve into something comparable? Will the Jewish community in Palestine someday acquire characteristics similar to those of the Christian communities in Lebanon? Will the declared objective of the PLO to set up a democratic, secular state in Palestine, in which Jews, Christians and Moslems will live side by side, be fulfilled this way — at some point in the future?

Because of the distinctive features of its communal set-up, Lebanon acquired a 'special functional role' in the whole Arab world. Will Israel too acquire a 'special functional role' in the region after a settlement is reached and the causes of friction removed? Obviously Israel's 'functional role' will never be the same as Lebanon's because of the unique Lebanese mosaic, its historical background, the nature of the various sects, etc. There is no question of Israel's performing the *same* 'functional role' as Lebanon but of its performing a very different role, similar to that of Lebanon only in so far as it will also have a functional character throughout the Arab world, after the settlement.

Certain parallels can be drawn between Lebanon's role in the Arab world and Switzerland's in Europe. Like Switzerland, Lebanon has responded to the needs and interests of neighbouring countries which they were either unable or unwilling, for various and sometimes conflicting reasons, to declare openly.[1]

Lebanon's banks have been a haven for private Arab capital; Lebanon was the playground for Arab tourists; Lebanon's press could say what the national press of other Arab countries could not. The Lebanese scene was an articulation of the controlled conflicts and interplay of political trends and ideas in the Arab world. Having no sources of income independent from its Arab neighbours, Lebanon was prosperous to the extent that it was both complementary to and different from the surrounding Arab environment. It is in this sense that Lebanon had a 'functional role' in the region and there is no question that Israel will one day acquire this same role.

Obviously it will not acquire any kind of 'functional role' in the region as long as it does not convince the Arab countries that it is no longer the embodiment of a project alien to their fate or directed against them. Israel can claim that it has always declared its readiness to perform such a role and that it was the Arabs who consistently and obstinately refused. In reply the Arabs can point to Israel's activity in Africa and prove that it aimed less at 'co-operation', 'complementarity' or, *a fortiori*, at 'integration', than it did at 'domination'. And certainly Israel's aims as regards the Arab world are more ambitious than its aims *vis-à-vis* Africa.

Israel in Africa

Israel exploited its unique situation as a country combining two features rarely found together in one state: its character as a 'developed country' belonging to the West in its human component and technological and scientific know-how; its character as an 'underdeveloped country', first by virtue of its location in the Third World at the crossroads of Asia and Africa and, secondly, because of the nature of the problems it faces in trying to adapt the Arab land it seized to the needs of the people it imported. It used its achievements to project the image of a successful experiment which was bound to attract those Third World countries which, unlike the Arabs, had not suffered from its usurpation of their land.

Israel took advantage of its affinity to the countries of the underdeveloped world to provide them with technical know-how which it portrayed as the product of its own successful experience as a sister African/Asian country.

Using its resources from the developed West — technical know-how, human expertise, and abundant capital — it could supply the underdeveloped world with more efficient and cheaper development models than the West, thanks to its experience in developing the Arab lands it settled. The imperialist West, and especially the United States, profited greatly from Israel's dealings with a large number of developing countries in whose eyes Israel was free from any taint of imperialism. It replaced the West, acting as a broker for western capital in deals which would otherwise have been suspect. Israel's prime benefit was her new role in many parts of Africa, which was likely to extend further to the rest of the Third World and circumscribe the Arab world from without.

In fact, with the help of the World Zionist Movement, Israel aspired to even more. There are indications that it strove to acquire certain features of a 'superpower'. This might appear an absurdity on the part of one of the smallest countries in the world, both in size and population, especially given that Israel's technical assistance to Africa never went beyond 0.5 per cent of all the aid received by that continent. Moreover, half this amount was furnished to Israel by external sources and its only role was to rechannel it to Africa. But Israel's aid to African countries was significant not quantitatively but qualitatively and in its selective character. This aid reveals Israel's real status at the core of contemporary imperialist structures. Israel does not squander its efforts but concentrates on nerve centres which are pinpointed with the aid of the best instruments the West possesses in the field of gathering and classification of information. In this domain Israel works in close co-operation with intelligence and espionage agencies, especially the CIA and academic and scientific organisations whose research is largely subsidised by the Agency.

Israel will definitely try to play a similar role in the Arab world as soon as the opportunity arises. However promising this role may have seemed in Africa, it ended adversely with a series of African countries severing their ties with Israel throughout 1973, reaching a climax during the October war. These boycotts may not have implied a rejection of Israeli aid *per se*, but expressed the solidarity of African countries with the Arab countries in condemning Israel's violation of the sovereignty of an African country and of Palestinian rights. In any case, the boycott indicated a growing African awareness that Israel was not a Third World country as it purported to be but belonged rather to the same category of countries as South Africa and Rhodesia and, like them, represented a threat to the unity of the African continent.

We have already said that the Arab-Israeli conflict could be reduced to a relationship between Israeli 'quality' and Arab 'quantity'. The same terms can be applied to Israel's relationship with the African countries except that no African territory had been usurped. Israel showed the sub-Saharan countries that it could provide them with aid on attractive terms and contribute to their development. She tried to make 'Israeli quality' complementary to 'African quantity', emphasising its ability to perform a 'functional role' in Africa's development. This attempt failed when the African countries realised that, even as it was striving towards this 'complementarity', Israel was violating the sovereignty of an African state.

The Possibility of an Israeli Function in the Middle East

After a settlement is reached in the Middle East, i.e. once a 'just peace' removing the original causes of the conflict is achieved, can Israel undertake a 'functional role' in the Arab world? But still the question remains: can the Arab countries accept this as beneficial to their development? Obviously the Arabs will not even consider this before all vestiges of their 25-year conflict with Israel are dissipated.

What is the main reason the conflict has gone on so long?

(1) Do the Arabs reject Israel because it is a Jewish state

implanted in the heart of the Islamic world? Such a tenet is widely invoked by influential religious circles both in the Islamic countries and in Israel. Yet not all Moslem countries boycott Israel. Iran and Turkey, for example, see Israel more as an enemy of the Arabs than as an enemy of Islam. The religious character of the conflict is stressed by obscurantists in both the Arab world and Israel. On the Moslem side, the theory should logically lead to the conclusion that Israel must be rejected from the Islamic world. In practice, even the most fundamentalist Arab countries no longer demand the eradication of Israel.

(2) Is the conflict basically national? If the Arabs accept this premise then it follows that all Jews constitute a national entity. It is not in the Arabs' interest to accept this premise, otherwise they would be adopting the basic Zionist thesis which justifies the establishment of a national home for the Jews in a land usurped from the Arabs.

Is the conflict national in another sense — a conflict between Arab nationalism on the one hand and Israeli, not Jewish, nationalism on the other? This could obviously not have been the original reason for the conflict because 'Israeli nationalism' did not exist at the time Israel was founded, its inhabitants being drawn from all over the world. But did it evolve into a national conflict in this sense after the relentless Arab-Israeli confrontation gave rise, as many contend, to an Israeli 'nationalism' or to an Israeli 'nation'? But if this were the reason it would not be basically different from many of the conflicts in modern history that have been solved by some means or other, e.g. France and Germany.

(3) Is the conflict over territory, over the fact that Zionism has built up a 'settlers' colony' in Palestine which has since expanded to encroach on the land of neighbouring Arab countries? A main reason for the conflict from the Arab viewpoint is the fact that Israel usurped Arab land, and transformed this territory into a 'sovereign state' whose sole means of preservation is *through* aggression and expansionism. The Arabs do not believe that this expansionist state is destined to survive. But the successive wars since the creation of Israel, including the 1973 war in which the Arabs achieved successes as in no previous war, carry convincing proof that Israel cannot be challenged solely or mainly by military means. Not only is this beyond Arab ability, at least within the current

balance of power, but is strongly condemned by world opinion. Even those who uphold the Arab cause are against it and any attempt to realise this aim could provoke a third world war.

What can be achieved is to curtail Israeli expansionism and to realise a peace in the region which recognises the right of all the conflicting parties to exist within secure and recognised borders, including the right of the Palestinian people to a homeland. There is thus a more or less tacit acknowledgement that the existence of Israel within secure and recognised borders is unavoidable after the Arabs recover their occupied territories and after the establishment of some Palestinian entity. What will then stand in the way of this acknowledgement evolving into an acceptance that Israel play a role in the region?

Perhaps for a long time the obstacle will be the Arab's feeling that Israeli 'quality' is a challenge to Arab 'quantity'. The Arabs had only one weapon to counter the supremacy of 'Israeli quality', the weapon of boycott, of not allowing Israel to play any kind of functional role in the Arab world. Perhaps the stumbling-block has always been the Arabs' fear of Israel's technological superiority and her ability, if peace came to the region, to dominate the Arabs economically and to prevent them from becoming masters of their own fate.

We must distinguish here between Israel's domination of the region as a foreign body grafted on to it and as a 'tool of imperialism'. There are many other strongholds of imperialism throughout the Arab world. Many Arab régimes see no threat to their independence or to the freedom of their political will from the new forms of imperialist interference. But even these régimes see Israel otherwise.

As we have seen there are many reasons why the conflict has not been solved but certainly one decisive reason why all Arab countries have refused any intercourse with Israel is that they fear Israeli technological and economic supremacy over the region. Even if a territorial settlement is concluded this would still remain a stumbling-block.

However, a new reality has emerged, namely that many aspects of Arab 'quantity' have acquired a 'qualitative' value. The proven ability of the Arabs to wage a highly efficient war, and the use of Arab oil and Arab capital have shattered Israel's economic and technological supremacy. After the October war, Israeli quality could no longer neutralise Arab quantity. In counterpart, Arab quantity could hold its own against Israeli quality. With the accumulation of capital, their capacity to purchase the trappings of modern technology and, what is more, their ability to develop their human capacities to respond to the needs of modern technology, the Arabs acquired a new confidence that Israeli superiority could no longer deprive them of their freedom of decision — even in the case of peace. Arab régimes no longer fear the removal of all barriers between them and Israel as much as they did in the past. In the light of these new realities, it is possible that certain Arab circles may come to think that Israel's technological and economic abilities could be an asset rather than a liability to Arab development?

For the first time some kind of match between Israeli technological know-how and Arab capital can be envisaged in certain quarters. Capital seeks technology just as the investment of technology requires available capital. Israel has always striven for this complementarity on which it bases its concept of inter-regional relations in the year 2000. It is a dream which the rich Jews of the Diaspora, the Zionist leaders and various western circles have always tried to induce the Arabs to consider. Edmond de Rothschild, along with a number of fellow Jewish millionaires, set up an institute in Switzerland immediately after the Arab defeat in 1967 to study the possibilities of contacting Arab business circles. This idea, which failed completely at the time, may not be rejected in the same way in the future. It may even be one of the forms taken by the rearrangement of contradictions in the region.

All the aspects of this 'complementarity' — if it is to come about — will certainly not be realised at one stroke. 'Security needs' might trigger the process. All security arrangements which have so far been devised to reinforce the settlement have been 'negative sanctions', like demilitarised zones or UN Emergency Forces. There has been no attempt yet to devise 'positive incentives' to promote the interest of the protagonists to abstain from war. Certain circles consider that one of the main incentives could be, for instance, a 'belt' of heavy industry on either side of the confrontation lines in the hope of dissuading all parties from exposing a lucrative industrial concentration to destruction.

Industrial projects could conceivably be set up in Sinai, in the Negev, the Gaza Strip, the West Bank, in various parts of a

Palestinian state, and even on the borders separating Israel from Syria and South Lebanon. Possibly petrochemical plants could be erected in some of these regions and more and more of the crude oil that now goes to the West could be retained to feed these petrochemical complexes. This Arab asset could be exported not in the form of crude alone but also in the form of finished and semi-finished products.

Setting up projects like this is tempting for more than one reason. They respond to the 'security requirements' of the various parties. The bid to reinforce security can attract the necessary capital for these sophisticated industries, which would in any case be less costly than present arms expenditures. This last consideration would overcome the reluctance of business circles to furnish huge sums just for development or to export modern industries which have hitherto been confined to the developed world.

Such developed industries (not necessarily limited to petro-chemicals) will also satisfy the pressing need of various countries in the region to dilute their concentration of population and to reclaim their deserts. These advanced industries could also include nuclear plants to desalinate sea-water for irrigating wide areas of the desert to meet growing food requirements. Egypt's pressing need to decongest its densely populated areas will also be met. Furthermore, industrial projects erected inside the Palestinian state will invalidate the argument that this state is not viable. Even today the Palestinians enjoy the highest *per capita* ratio of qualified personnel in the Arab world.

It is clear that security needs can be a springboard for intercourse across the borders between Israel and its neighbours in the future. This could extend to a wider area of the Arab world; once it is accepted in principle, some Arabs could go so far as to contemplate two distinct phases after the settlement: a first phase in which they could seek the help of the international community to 'tame' Israel and to absorb it into the region; a second phase in which they could use Israeli human and technological assets to achieve a Middle East conglomerate able to stand up to the big geographical conglomerates expected to coalesce at the turn of the century.

This might appear to some as the ideal projection for the rearrangement of contradictions in the region. However, history is seldom free of contradictions, especially when it faces contradictions as deep as the Arab-Israeli conflict. Other outcomes are certainly more likely.

A first stumbling-block would be Israel's attempts to break up the settlement into a number of separate agreements. It will certainly try to achieve a settlement only with those Arab parties it believes should be reckoned with, in the hope that partial agreements will drive wedges between the Arabs and will allow Israel to neutralise the weaker links instead of dealing with all Arab parties as equals. Though Israel might see immediate benefits in this, in the long run it carries a serious threat. It will not eliminate the 'vertical' contradictions between the protagonists, nor will it restore stability to the region. Such a situation is bound to threaten these partial agreements and carries strong reasons for the resumption of hostilities.

But even if a total settlement is achieved there will be a problem concerning Israel itself. The only justification for its existence is as the embodiment of the Zionist design, and it would lose its *raison d'être* if its role is reduced to that of an economic instrument that the Arab environment would have digested and used for its own development.

It is true that Israel has already been an economic instrument on behalf of various international parties, especially world imperialism. As has been mentioned, Israel performed this role in Africa where it acted as a broker for world monopolies. Since its inception Israel has continuously tried to play a similar role in the Arab world. It failed not for want of trying but because the Arabs consistently resisted this. Thus Israel does not object in principle to being an economic instrument in the service of other parties. This has always been a means to an end — the consolidation of the Zionist design. However, that this should replace its original identity as the embodiment of the Zionist design is quite another matter.

Can Israel reconcile its original identity and its potential as an economic instrument serving Arab development? This role will suit the neo-imperialist strategy re-adapted to the rise in oil prices and the expected increase in prices of other strategic raw materials. In these new conditions imperialism will find it more advantageous to export industries than to import raw materials. The distribution of these industries will be carried out on the basis of the proximity of the relevant source of raw material to an industry, in order to curtail prices and limit pollution of the industrialised world. But Israel's very foundations might be shaken by this new 'functional role'. The Arabs will never accept it as the embodiment of the Zionist design. Its obstinacy in refusing a settlement might rekindle anti-Semitism throughout the world. Would this not strengthen its resolve to cling to the Zionist dream? And if a settlement is reached, many Arab Jews will eventually return to their original homelands. Will they go as Israeli emissaries or end up by resettling? Israel has always derived its strength by claiming that its very existence was at stake. Can it continue to obtain foreign aid once this argument loses credibility? To what extent can Israel stand up to such a transformation? Israel's acquiring a functional role in the region would be a decisive victory of the doves. Will the hawks, who have always been the real policy-makers in Israel, give in to this? Even its function as an economic instrument in its environment depends upon its remaining a source of sophisticated know-how and capital. This may disappear if its original identity ceases to be and its ties with influential and wealthy circles outside the region are severed.

All these dilemmas facing Israel indicate that the Palestinian dream to erect a secular democratic state extending to the whole of Palestine is not chimeric and it could very well be peace rather than war that could transform this dream into reality.

For these reasons, Israel will resist being absorbed into the region with all the means at its disposal. That is why a fifth war is likely. That is why Israel will take advantage of every loophole and every chance to assert its identity against the threat of being digested by its environment. It will do everything in its power to prevent Arab cohesion and the increase of Arab weight and cogency. To this end it will stand with any force inside the Arab world or on its periphery that has the same interest in weakening and splintering the Arab nation. For example, it may seek an alliance with Iran against Saudi Arabia and will try to stir up any possible future conflict over the Gulf. It will incite all separatist movements in the Arab world, such as encouraging the Kurds against Baghdad's central authority or the separatist movement in southern

Sudan.

But Israel's main effort will more likely be inside the Arab world itself, where it will try to stabilise reactionary or pro-western régimes and oppose progressive and revolutionary trends. It will counter the Soviet Union's influence in the Arab world and will blackmail it into allowing greater emigration of Soviet Jews. In short, Israel is expected to be the Trojan Horse in the heart of the Arab nation on behalf of neo-imperialism. This could lead to an internal breakdown in Israel, undermining it as the embodiment of the Zionist design, reducing its effectiveness as an instrument for neo-imperialism, in short, to its collapse.

Post-settlement perspectives do not imply the disappearance of contradictions but, on the contrary, imply that Israel will play a major role in intensifying 'horizontal' contradictions where previously its role was concentrated on intensifying the 'vertical' ones.

NOTE

1. Since the Arabic version of this book was published, far from being a model for Palestine, the communal set-up in Lebanon has collapsed. This does not necessarily invalidate the notion of multireligious states in the Middle East. It is rather an expression of the 'rearrangement of contradictions' in the region which generates chaos more easily than peace if the new set-up is misunderstood. Because of Lebanon's extremely sensitive equilibrium, it was the first to experience such a breakdown.

Conclusion

This study has focused on some basic questions: How far has détente influenced the Arab-Israeli conflict? To what extent has a settlement now become possible, after the October war made the rules of détente applicable to the Middle East crisis by introducing, for the first time, commensurability between the principals? In other words, to what extent can what we have termed the 'rearrangement of contradictions' on the global level be applied to the Middle East crisis? Can this specific regional crisis find a solution in terms of principles derived from the present global crisis-solving techniques?

Détente is closely related to peaceful coexistence between conflicting social systems, as illustrated by the new US/USSR equation. The Middle East crisis, on the other hand, is basically a question of national liberation, symbolised in the rejection of a prominent manifestation of colonialism in its most literal sense: 'colon' imperialism.

In terms of contemporary international legality, buttressed by détente, forcing a people to relinquish the land to which they belong is alien to the idea of justice. Neither the states belonging to the socialist world nor those belonging to the capitalist world are required, under détente, to relinquish land. Détente in fact legalised the *status quo* situation which came about after World War Two, and which was codified but not always respected in the conventions concluded after the war, especially in the UN Charter. Contrary to the pattern which prevailed during the Cold War, all changes must now stem from within each country, according to the will of its own people, and any interference from without is bound to threaten détente.

This condition does not apply to Israel, which was established in Palestine against the will of the Palestinians after the end of World War Two and after the promulgation of the UN Charter. From this viewpoint, the properties of the Middle East crisis as a whole, and not only those of the Palestinian-Israeli conflict, are in opposition to those inherent in détente, as the issue here is over land seized from the Arabs.

This book has stressed that Israel should not be looked upon as a phenomenon of a purely colonial or racial character. It has deliberately departed from the prevalent Arab view, which tends to overemphasise certain of Israel's attributes and to overlook others. The Arabs have been as radical in their verbal denigration of Israel as they have been deficient in their action against it. But that is not to say that Israel is unrelated to imperialism. Its link with imperialism was blatantly expressed by the founder of Zionism, Theodor Herzl: 'We shall be a rampart against Asia, an outpost for civilization against the barbarians.' Civilisation for Europe at the end of the last century meant European civilisation, i.e. European imperialism. And for European imperialism at that time, the barbarians meant the downtrodden peoples resisting colonial rule.

It can be said in general that any European colonial scheme in the twentieth century for settling Europeans in areas that were subjected to colonial rule acquires a colonialist character, whatever the motivations of the settlers and irrespective of the reactions of the natives. This is all the more true in the case of the Zionist design, which initiated resistance since it first set up Jewish settlements in Palestine several decades before the promulgation of the Balfour Declaration.

The implementation of the Zionist design was closely related to the rise of imperialism at the end of the last century. It concurred with European imperialism's assault on the collapsing Ottoman Empire. Israel's creation goes back to an unjustified gesture of sovereignty made by Great Britain on 2 November 1917, when Lord Balfour made his famous Declaration to Lord Rothschild: 'His Majesty's Government looks with favour upon the establishment of a national home for the Jewish people in Palestine.'

When the White Paper was issued in 1939, the Jews claimed that Britain was imposing restrictions on their immigration at a time when persecution of Europe's Jews had reached a climax under Hitler. However, the terrorism practised in protest by such Zionist organisations as Irgun and Stern against the mandate authorities did not mean that the Jewish resistance to the British Mandate acquired the character of a 'war of liberation' against British colonialism. Nor did the Jewish resistance deprive the Arabs' resistance to the establishment of

Israel in 1948 of its character as a liberation movement aiming to repel settler colonialism and its usurpation of Arab lands.

The Zionist design materialised, and Israel came into being under the aegis of imperialism. Thus Israel's existence is organically linked to colonialism, to the prevalence of traditional imperialism. Will Israel survive if imperialism is to vanish? What will Israel's fate be now that traditional colonialism is being replaced by more insidious forms, better adapted to the requirements of the present balance of power, illustrated by imperialism's acceptance of peaceful coexistence with the socialist world?

Israel's connection with imperialism is somewhat ambiguous. In formal terms Israel came into being as the embodiment of the Zionist design, which has its own properties and its specific objectives, not all of which are imputable to colonialism. Although opinions may differ as to whether the Jews should desert their original homelands, the fact remains that a great many of them in various parts of the world have responded to the Zionist call. This might be due to the fact that, unlike other minorities, the Jews were not wholly integrated in most European societies. Another reason is the persecution and discrimination they suffered in the unenlightened European societies like Czarist Russia, which culminated in their mass extermination under Nazism.

By and large, persecution and discrimination of the Jews was intensified with the growing omnipotence of imperialism, despite the fact that Jewish-accumulated experience in trade and finance brought Jewish capitalism into the key positions of contemporary monopoly capitalism.

Jewish settler colonialism in Palestine is different from traditional settler imperialism not only because it springs from the injustice and persecution suffered by the Jews but also because the Jews who emigrated to Palestine came from many different countries and not from one colonial country, like the French settlers in Algeria or the settlers of British and Dutch origin in Rhodesia and South Africa. This ambiguity has made it difficult for the Arabs to convince many non-Arabs that Israel is nothing but a bridgehead of colonialism. Also because of this ambiguity, the Arab-Israeli conflict resisted, more than any other issue of our time, the changes that have occured since the onset of détente. Until the October war at least it was characterised by inveterate antagonism and was ruled by the laws of the Cold War.

This disassociation between Israel and imperialism might be justified, even desirable, for tactical political purposes, but is certainly unacceptable conceptually and in general strategic terms.

Even if it is valid to assume that imperialism as an international phenomenon will not disappear in the near future, this should not prevent the formulation of a vision of the future of the Arab-Israeli conflict in the absence of imperialism and with the assumption of an end to its interference. Otherwise all expectations concerning the ultimate projection of this conflict would remain incomplete and faulty.

If imperialism maintains that the time is now opportune for a settlement, it is because it realises that the Arab-Israeli conflict in its conventional form — that of endless strike — no longer suits its interests to the same extent in the new world climate. For in a climate of peaceful coexistence and world détente, imperialism is no longer free to resort to overt military intervention to protect the more conspicuous forms of neo-colonialist exploitation which have become necessary since the accession to political independence by the bulk of former colonies in the early sixties. One main target is to check the attempts of the underdeveloped countries to bridge the widening gap between the prices of manufactured goods produced by advanced capitalist countries and those of strategic raw materials, which are the underdeveloped countries' source of income. The rise in oil prices following the October war was a first attempt. In general, the adjustment of prices of strategic raw materials constitutes a severe blow to this prominent new source of exploitation. Fierce rounds in this battle can be anticipated in the coming years, especially if the climate of world détente is to be safeguarded.

Hence imperialism must devise new methods to face its economic crisis and to maintain the essence of exploitation. It no longer opposes transfer of some unsophisticated industries to developing countries, especially those polluting the environment, those requiring easily assimilated technology or abundant and cheap manpower, in exchange for ensuring the flow of strategic raw materials, foremost among which is oil. The aim is to foster capitalism in developing countries and prevent developments on non-capitalist lines.

For example, in order to resist nationalisation in the Arab world, the world's greatest reservoir of oil, imperialism no longer opposes some new forms of 'partnership'. To resist the domination of the public sector in the economy, it no longer insists on its formal liquidation but tries rather to deprive it of its leading role. To prevent the Arab countries from following the road of their choice to their development — a delicate task for imperialism after it has admitted the necessity of a global redistribution of industrialisation and at a time when Arab oil surpluses have reached astronomical figures — it finds it necessary to devise new means to maintain its control over Arab oil assets. These include encouraging the trend towards recycling the surplus through the advanced capitalist countries, using it to flood world monetary markets to ensure international monetary fluidity and to equilibrate the developed capitalist countries' balance of payments. It also encourages assigning Arab surplus capital for the purchase of land and the development of real estate ownership abroad and to tourism projects. It favours, moreover, the use of this capital in speculation, even for short-term blocked accounts, rather than its use for the development of the Arab world according to an overall plan over which it would have less control. This is why Kissinger is so keen on keeping the strings of the settlement in his own hands, and also why EEC countries are so eager for a Euro-Arab dialogue.

This signifies that the Arab-Israeli conflict in the form prevalent during the last quarter-century can become a liability for imperialism, seriously threatening its interests in the whole region. Hence the need in the view of various business quarters for Israel to assume the role of the 'maison d'expertise' in the region, rather than to continue as the policeman for imperialism.

This *maison d'expertise* will be entrusted with overseeing the area's development, keeping it within the range that would not jeopardise imperialism's designs. In this sense the settlement involves the launching of a new role for Israel.

The Arab-Israeli conflict, within the context of the conventional imperialist design, has been characterised by absolute incompatibility between 'Israel quality' and 'Arab quantity'. The new imperialist design, on the other hand, requires the replacement of this incompatibility by complementarity. Thus while it was the hawks in Israel who had to have the 'longer arm' under the previous design, under the new design the doves are to come to the fore.

Thus imperialism has been keen on encouraging a degree of commensurability between the principals to the dispute in order to pave the way to a settlement. In so doing its aim is to affect the necessary 'shock' that would lead to the rearrangement of contradictions in a manner serving its interest best. For this reason, imperialism would not oppose approaches to the conflict depriving it of its social content, approaches that would promote 'common denominators' and a new 'common language'.

This does not mean however that if imperialism and right-wing forces are interested in a settlement the left should oppose it *a priori*. This abrupt change in imperialism's strategy denotes the bankruptcy of its previous trend, which it is relinquishing under pressure. Resisting neo-imperialism does not presuppose rejecting a settlement in principle, thus exposing the region and the world at large to grave risks, but requires rather the harnessing of these new realities to the benefit of progressive forces.

Imperialism no longer enjoys unchallenged control over enormous capital which can now be geared to the development of Arab land thanks to Arab solidarity cemented by the blood of the October war. However, such an investment is difficult if Arab surplus is regarded by each of the oil-producing countries as its own individual property and not as part of one unified, comprehensive scheme treating this development as an integral whole. This surplus is bound to dry up sooner or later, with the drying up of Arab oil or the drying up of its function as a source of energy. It is therefore imperative that the Arabs convert their oil from a raw material into finished or semi-finished products with lasting value. The prevention of Arab oil becoming the source of individual wealth and not of the nation's development as a whole is a task entrusted to the Arab left in the broad sense of the word.

The relationship between the 'Middle East crisis' and the 'energy crisis' appeared to be at first a random one. The fact that the world's most important reservoir of oil happened to be located in countries belonging to the same Arab nation as those exposed to Israeli occupation appeared to be an accident of history. But the oil war, which sustained the achievements of the October war on the battlefield, has proved that the two issues are not separate. In fact, they are two facets of the same struggle. One facet, the oil issue, represents Arab liberation from a prominent form of contemporary *economic* imperialism while the other, the October war, represents Arab *political* liberation from a prominent form of settler imperialism. Both are closely knit into one battle against the domination of imperialism over the destiny of the area.

Aware of this correlation between the two facets, imperialism seeks to use the outcome of the one to affect the outcome of the other. Hence its keenness to replace Israel's traditional role by a new one. Even if this new role will entail a settlement involving Israeli withdrawal from occupied Arab territory, it will be designed with a view to ensuring imperialism's economic hegemony over the area.

It is incumbent on the left, more than on any other trend, to thwart the negative aspects of this new rationale and to further promote the positive achievements of the Arab liberation movement. Once Israel's expansionist aims are checked, the left must carry the battle further on both the economic and political fronts at one and the same time.

Throughout the fifties and sixties, the Arab revolution struggled to turn the political independence wrested from conventional imperialism into the nucleus of a strong economic potential. A socio-economic structure based on a public sector was set up, aimed at harnessing available resources for development and unleashed a process through which society gradually freed itself from imperialism and capitalism. This process is still under way in specific Arab countries.

The left in the seventies should formulate a new strategy for the Arab revolution in order to tackle an apparently opposite task — how to make the most out of the Arab economic potential resulting from the readjustment in oil prices in order to further promote political independence, this time not only within specific Arab countries but on a Pan-Arab scale. Should this be achieved, the breakaway of the Arab nation as a whole from imperialism and world capitalism will be assured.

In spite of the apparent opposition in the Arab revolution's task before and after the October war, it is the same in essence, in fact its new features result from the rearrangement of contradictions on both the international and regional levels. This rearrangement of contradictions requires a new *modus operandi*. Exactly as the opposition between imperialism and capitalism on the one hand and socialism on the other is no longer marked by the division of the world community into two antagonistic camps, so the struggle for development and liberation throughout the Arab nation will not preserve the feature of a group of progressive Arab states in confrontation with a group of conservative ones.

Throughout the unfolding of this process in the future, two 'moments' could be foreseen: a first 'moment' where the new Arab weapons, Arab oil and Arab capital, are expected to gain momentum, invigorating capitalism and giving the impression that capitalism can realise development all over the Arab region — the negation of the past thirty years; a second 'moment', which will 'negate' the 'negation' and prove once again that no real development to the benefit of the Arab peoples is possible within an economic framework over which imperialism and world capitalism regain the upper hand.

Revolutionary phenomena similar to those experienced by specific Arab countries during the last two decades are bound to come to the fore once again, but this time on a higher level encompassing the whole Arab nation. By still further developing progressive Pan-Arabism and promoting the integration of the Arab community, these phenomena will sever the Arab world' links with imperialism and capitalism, gaining in the process the neutralisation of Israel as an obstacle to these objectives.

What would Israel's fate be then? Can it preserve its identity as an embodiment of the Zionist project and protect it throughout the first 'moment', the moment of the settlement, with its implication that Israel may acquire a function in the surrounding Arab environment? Can it retain this function in the second 'moment', with the ebb of imperialism which secured its privileged status within this environment? Or will it wither away to become only a focus of Jewish culture, whose undeniable contribution to the heritage of mankind could become an asset to the region's development once freed from all taint of manipulation and exploitation? After all, the Jews have always enjoyed tolerance throughout the Arabs' long history, contrary to the harsh treatment they received in Europe. Thanks to this tolerance, many great Jewish thinkers emerged like Saadeya and Maimonides, Saladin's physician and a student of Averoes.

In fact, only the left can substantiate the Arabs' resolution not to let the settlement become an abandonment of their ends but simply a readjustment of their means. From this optic, the Zionist scheme will perish at its zenith. The very instant of its completion will signal its extinction. But history is never linear. Though this optic charts the logical course of future moments, seldom does history unfold without digressions and imponderables which blur its main course.

We have identified two 'moments': the first, a negation of the promises of the Arab revolution; the second, a negation of the negation, i.e. a reassertion of the Arab revolution through a negation of the aspiration of Arab wealth. The first can include a settlement with Israel, the second presages the fading away of Israel into the Arab landscape. The sequence in these two 'moments' is logical, not necessarily chronological, as the future can be predicted in terms of content, not of form. This content is still furiously resisted by various trends: the hawks in Israel and the 'rejectionists' in the Arab world.

So singular are the features of the Arab-Israeli conflict that it may seem at first glance to be out of phase with the major conflicts of our time. A more penetrating look will reveal that, more than many other conflicts, it can enrich our comprehension of the age in which we live.

Postscript

Throughout the last year this book has provoked an uproar in the Arab world. This postscript will discuss the most germane of the various accusations that have been levelled against it.

1. *It has been argued that the book's approach is one-sided. It overrates the role of external factors (détente, the superpowers, oil) and underrates the intrinsic elements of the conflict. More important, coming from an Arab writer, it belittles the achievements of the Arab liberation movement and the victories scored the world over against its enemy, American imperialism.*

It is the deep-felt opinion in the Arab world that Israel and the Arabs are totally irreconcilable and no external factor can change this. Although the book deliberately departs from this outlook it does not deny that the ultimate goals of the protagonists are incompatible nor that the intensity and relentlessness of the conflict exceed all others in the region. However, these features do not justify treating the conflict as though it were a category apart, immune from the influence of the political environment. In fact, as we have seen, the Arabs do acknowledge implicitly that the conflict is affected by the environment, if only because they regard it as part of an Arab liberation struggle against imperialism which they admit has gone through several stages with different features in the last twenty-five years.

This book's focus on détente has puzzled the Arab world because in common with many Europeans the Arabs have not yet grasped the full significance of détente. It is more one-sided to ignore détente than discuss it, because its implications go far beyond mutual relations between the superpowers. However, the process of détente is still evolving. A year ago, when this book was written, the most noticeable feature of détente was superpower intervention from 'above', more specifically

American manipulation of the conflict determined by the growing importance of oil in its global strategy. Since then another aspect of détente has become more apparent, namely, a wider spectrum of conflict emerging not from the summit, but from the base of international community. This complex array of conflicts erupting from 'below' has started to impinge on the Arab-Israeli conflict. This explains the growing impact of the Palestinian issue in the international arena in spite of periodic crackdowns on Palestinians in the Arab world. It also explains the recent UN resolution equating Zionism with racism. This is what we meant by the Palestinian issue acquiring dimensions going beyond its original character as the core of the Arab-Israeli dispute, becoming more and more an inspiration for the revolt of the dispossessed against the affluent, both in its ends and in its means. The Palestinian struggle is becoming a catalyst in the confrontation between the haves and the have-nots. The Arab-Israeli conflict was always a crisis point in the confrontation between East and West throughout the Cold War period. If there is no settlement in the near future, with détente, it could become a crisis point in the growing confrontation between North and South.

2. *Many have criticised the book for lacking commitment. This is appropriate to the style of western game-playing, but it is incompatible with an Arab nationalist stand, still less with a Marxist class approach. The book uses conceptual tools of a neutral character such as quality and quantity, commensurability and parity, the rearrangement of contradictions. This categorisation of the ingredients of the conflict ignore its basic character as a confrontation between Arab national and social liberation on one hand and world imperialism on the other.*

It is sometimes necessary to stand back from the traditional partisan position so that a wider perspective of the realities of the conflict can strengthen this position. Détente has made this especially true. Once weapons were produced capable of destroying the globe the big powers had no choice but to freeze certain modes of conflict like nuclear warfare. This mechanism of freezing certain modes of conflict requires that the parties admit a certain parity. Now parity between parties of opposed ideology introduces the need for some common measure, for some basis for comparison, between qualitatively different things. No such common measure can be conceived from an exclusively partisan stand. This has been true for the SALT negotiations, where stockpiles of strategic weapons of a qualitatively different category had to be compared. It is also true in the negotiations for European security, where the equation is much more complex given the multiplicity and diversity of the parties involved. This will also have to be true for a settlement in the Middle East, where the problem is no less intricate and complex. In these agreements between the superpowers or on the European level, no party has ever been seriously accused of abandoning its basic philosophy, its ultimate goals or its partisan stand. Using conceptual tools of a neutral character is condemnable only when no effort is subsequently made to reintegrate the abstract analysis into its national and social context.

3. *It does not follow that because the Arabs have achieved some sort of parity with Israel a settlement is necessarily forthcoming. On the contrary, this should be an additional incentive to press the struggle forward towards an ultimate Arab victory.*

There can be no question of a total victory before parity is achieved and the balance of power moves in the Arabs' favour. But once the scales tip, the means of achieving total victory need not be the same as before, when the Arabs had to resort to war to restore their rights. The case for a settlement is that it would prevent Israel from resorting to war to upset this new Arab advantage. This is all the more justified since détente has established ground rules for the settlement of conflict situations that do not require that protagonists abandon their ultimate goals.

4. *The book's use of neutral conceptual tools is misleading because they focus on the similarities in the structural aspects and conceal the differences in the processes which produce them. An obvious example is the book's use of the concept of 'rearrangement of contradictions' to define both détente and a Middle East settlement, without making clear a basic*

difference: whereas in the case of détente the rearrangement of contradictions has been a setback for imperialism which had to renounce the Cold War for peaceful coexistence, in the Arab-Israeli conflict the settlement as a rearrangement of contradictions could, on the contrary, be an outcome of a neo-colonialist master plan to re-adapt imperialism's presence in the region to the new structural build-up. By concealing this difference, the book paves the way for this master plan at the expense of the Arab liberation movement.

The Arab liberation movement has no control over the rearrangement of contradictions at the summit nor on the impact of the détente process on various conflict situations, including the Middle East Thus, however different the process of détente from the mechanism of a settlement in the Middle East, similarities still hold to the extent that the course of the Arab-Israeli conflict is affected by détente. To resist the detrimental aspects of this impact, it is necessary to be aware *how* it will affect the course of the conflict. To predict is not to advocate. Charting a very likely course of the game of contradictions serves the interests of the Arab liberation movement, for it is through awareness of the critical eventualities that these interests can be best safeguarded.

5. *Vertical and horizontal contradictions, i.e. national and social contradictions, should not be regarded as mutually exclusive. On the contrary, they are complementary. Thanks to the acuteness of the national aspect in the Arab-Israeli conflict, revolutionary social processes have been stimulated in the Arab world and, reciprocally, social transformation cannot acquire its full scope if the national struggle is aborted or frozen.*

Indeed, national and social contradictions are complementary. But they are also distinct. It is true that revolutionary social processes were stimulated by the national aspect in the Arab-Israeli conflict. But it is also true that the acuteness of this national aspect was used to justify freezing certain modes of social contradiction. This is implicit in slogans like: 'the voice of the battle must drown any other'.

Though in the case of a settlement, the national contradiction would be frozen, the social contradictions which will erupt within the various parties to the dispute will become the main vehicle for the pursuit of the national goals. That is the meaning the book gives to the substitution of the horizontal (social) contradictions in place of the vertical (national) ones as the most prominent form of contradiction once a settlement is reached.

6. *It is hard to see how Israel could acquire a functional role in the region if one begins from the premise that Israeli-Zionist objectives and those of the Arab world are basically irreconcilable. How can the Arabs adopt the basic objective of Zionism, which has always been to create a role for Israel in the region?*

The book advocates no reconciliation between the two outlooks. If Israel is to acquire a functional role in the region, it will be on the basis of the horizontal contradictions. Complementarity between Arab capital and Israeli know-how means nothing more than a reconciliation between Arab right-wing forces and Zionism within the framework of a neo-imperialist master plan. In opposition to this, one cannot exclude that throughout the settlement process the Arab revolutionary movement and anti-Zionist forces, even within Israel, will wage a common struggle against this master plan. This common struggle is the only solid basis for the survival of a Jewish community in Palestine and its integration into the region. The catalyst of this transformation is the Palestinian freedom struggle.

With the new dimensions it is now acquiring, the possibilities open before the Palestinian struggle are much greater than one would tend to believe. That is why Security Council resolution 242, a product of the balance of power in the aftermath of the 1967 Arab defeat, which does not take into account the dimensions which the Palestinian issue has since acquired, seems to be now *dépassé*. Nor does the Partition Plan of 1947, which also derives its legitimacy from a previous United Nations resolution, seem to be the most suitable basis for a solution now that détente has established ground rules that do not require either side in a conflict situation to give up its ultimate goals.

The PLO should be included in the negotiation process without requiring its recognition of Israel as a precondition.

The classical example of the relationship between the two superpowers since détente is not the best precedent. True, although the Soviet Union has not renounced its ultimate goal of building Communism the world over, and the US has not renounced its goal of eradicating Communism, peaceful coexistence between them is possible. But while the notion of peaceful coexistence can apply to the relationship between the socialist and capitalist worlds, it cannot apply to the confrontation between national liberation movements and imperialism. Furthermore, security borders are clearly established between the East and the West, which is not the case in the Arab-Israeli conflict where Israel still occupies substantial areas of Arab territory far beyond the historical borders of Palestine.

A better example is that of the Vietnam negotiations in Paris which included four parties: the US, the Hanoi government, the Saigon government and the Provisional Revolutionary government of South Vietnam. Neither the PRG nor Hanoi recognised the Saigon government and vice versa. Nor was there mutual recognition between the PRG and Hanoi on one side and the US on the other. But this was no obstacle for negotiations going on over long years in spite of bitter fighting in Vietnam. These negotiations culminated in the famous Paris Agreements which were a turning point towards a solution of the Vietnamese problem. The parties agreed not to agree on the substance of the dispute. Agreement was confined to procedural rules for mutually acceptable modes of conflict without requiring any of the parties to give up their ultimate goals.

The cases of Vietnam and Palestine are not identical. The principal enemy for the Vietnamese was an external enemy, the US, while for the Palestinians it is an internal enemy settled inside Palestine, Israel. This will make the ultimate solution of the Palestinian-Israeli issue a much longer historical process. But this difference does not make the ground rules of the Vietnamese settlement inapplicable to an eventual settlement of the core of the Arab-Israeli dispute.[1]

NOTE

1. If as a condition for reaching a settlement, the Palestinian issue should acquire precedence over the other issues, the question of Jerusalem should be the last to be tackled. A holy city for the three great religions, Jerusalem's importance goes beyond the question of territorial gain. Once all other issues are settled, international law could come up with an appropriate formula acceptable to all parties concerned.

Appendix: A Blueprint for Breaking the Basic Impasse

This is an abridged version of a paper presented by the author to the 'Palestine Colloquium' held in Brussels from 13 to 15 May 1976 under the title 'The Right of the Palestinians to Self-determination'. Along the lines of this book, it is an attempt to overcome the basic difficulty that still obstructs a breakthrough towards peace.

Two obstacles hamper a genuine application of the principle of self-determination to the Palestinians: the implantation of the Zionist state of Israel in a part of Palestine and the resultant uprooting of a considerable portion of the original Palestinian inhabitants. The right of every people to self-determination is indivisible: it cannot be applied to a fraction of a people or to a fraction of the land in which they have their roots. This is all the more true now that Israeli occupation deprives the Palestinians of any independent existence in any part of Palestine.

The Palestinian problem is the nucleus of the Arab-Israeli conflict. The aggravation of the conflict and its extension beyond the boundaries of Palestine have not resulted in blurring it. On the contrary, it has been further promoted and matured and any settlement which avoids facing it is no longer conceivable.

That is why the implementation of Security Council Resolution 242 has not materialised. Drawn up in the aftermath of the Arab débâcle of June 1967, it reflected a balance of power which no longer holds true. It treated the Palestinian problem as a problem of refugees, of individual evictees, and not as a problem of a people with a right to self-determination.

That is also why the step-by-step diplomacy inaugurated by Kissinger in the aftermath of the October 1973 war becomes inoperative beyond a certain point. Not only does it deliberately defer the Palestinian issue indefinitely but, precisely for this reason, it has proved inadequate also in arriving at a solution of the problem of occupied Arab territories outside the boundaries of Palestine. For even if we were to believe Israel's claim that its intention is to assure its survival and not its expansion (a claim belied by Israel's overt or creeping annexationism), clinging to the occupied territories provides it with a trump card. Indeed, Israel has expressed its willingness to give up part of these occupied territories inasmuch as a partial pull-back would adapt its defence system better to the new realities of the post-October war situation: to the extent, for instance, that the collapse of the Bar-Lev line requires a substitute, or in so far as America's increased interest in the new Arab oil assets will eventually induce her to use her leverage over Israel to effect withdrawal. But as long as the Israelis perceive Palestinian aspirations as a threat to the very integrity of their state, why should they give up their trump card? The final evacuation of Arab occupied territories and the settling of the Palestinian problem are two organically linked issues.

And so we still confront a total deadlock. However, it would be wrong to deny that the October war has introduced new elements. By establishing a certain parity between the belligerents, the war contributed towards removing many of the inhibitions which prevented the very idea of a negotiation process. The war initiated a movement towards a settlement. Significant though this movement may have been, it did not acquire sufficient momentum to carry it to complete fulfilment. This gave rise to a precarious situation which retained neither the features of the previous polarisation nor those which a stable peace would establish instead. This situation was made even more precarious by the process of successive and separate disengagements which American diplomacy opted for. And as tension was reduced on one front beyond the threshold that other Arab fronts could tolerate, it became intolerable elsewhere. It flared up within the Arab world rather than in face of Israel. Lebanon, which had hitherto testified to the viability of a Mideastern multi religious society, exploded. Moreover, the harrassment which the Palestinians are now being subjected to in Lebanon justifies the belief that even if American diplomacy succeeds in achieving a second disengagement on the Golan after Sinai, this new step will, far from benefiting the Palestinian cause, expose it to still greater beleaguerment.

The fact is that for American diplomacy the Palestinian problem is a difficulty to sidestep, a detonator to defuse, and not a national issue for which a just solution must be found.

Every US initiative towards the Arabs, beginning with the Rogers plan, has been detrimental to the Palestinian resistance. This first intervention was rapidly followed by the eviction of the Palestinians from Jordan. The crackdown was the most brutal yet. The train of events since then has never disproved the fact that the more the US became the key element in the struggle towards a settlement, the more tightly was the net pulled on the *fedayeen* by some third party; there was never a question of a genuine recognition of the Palestinians' right to self-determination. Until today, the US is the only relevant party in the international arena not to recognise the PLO or to admit 'legitimate rights' to the Palestinians, but only 'legitimate interests'. If the Palestinians lacked nothing but 'legitimate interests', while not one square inch of Palestinian territory is submitted to a sovereign Palestinian authority, the Palestinian people will never attain their right to self-determination.

Why does the US so obstinately refuse all sovereign rights to the Palestinians at the same time that it is trying to normalise its relations with the rest of the Arab world, and aspires to the leading role in settling the Arab-Israeli dispute? Why is it that whenever the right of the Palestinians to self-determination comes up, it remains an elusive and ambiguous slogan?

An argument often presented, even by the Arabs' friends here in Europe and in the USA, is that the Israeli fact cannot be exclusively attributed to a colonial or purely racist phenomenon, and that its survival is justified in so far as it has been the product not only of colonisation of an ethnic or racist character, but also of the racial persecution suffered by the Jews throughout the centuries which culminated in their near extermination under Hitler. Thus Israel has a right to exist. This is a moral right, not a right which Israel acquired only through its military superiority. Of course our European friends will add that this right should not eclipse the Palestinians' right to self-determination — not only because the Palestinians are not responsible for the persecution of the Jews. As these two rights, Israeli and Palestinian, are irreconcilable and each, by its very nature, negates the other, as we cannot partition the right, we have no choice therefore but to partition the land.

This argument is a fallacy. In terms of logic, it derives from a correct premise (namely, the basic incompatibility of the two rights) a conclusion that it presents as the *only* deduction that can be drawn from this premise (namely, the partition of the land), while in fact this conclusion is not the only possible one — at least in theory. A partition of Palestine can imply a partition in the space dimension, i.e. a partition of the *land*. It can also imply a partition in the time dimension, i.e. the assertion of either of these two rights at a *given historical moment*. This hypothesis is not purely theoretical, it has been the case of Palestinian history throughout long millennia.

It can be argued that to retain this second hypothesis instead of the first, i.e. to propose replacing Israel by a Palestinian state instead of striving for the establishment of two states in Palestine, one Israeli and the other Arab, is to scuttle all chances of peace in the Middle East. That it is in fact perpetuating the conflict until its ultimate denouement, which is to eventually eliminate one of the two conflicting parties, with ever more serious implications for world peace. This accusation is levelled against certain contingents of the Palestinian resistance, particularly those of the rejectionist front. And even if the tendency described as 'realistic' or 'moderate' in the leadership of the PLO came to recognise Israel in return for Israeli recognition of the PLO, doubts are raised as to the ability of this tendency to preserve its representativeness of Palestinian legitimacy, if only because restricting the Palestinian right to self-determination to a fraction of Palestinian territory is in itself an aberration of self-determination. Sooner or later, this concession will be challenged and peace threatened. These are the apprehensions by which American diplomacy seeks to justify its boycott of the PLO, encourages repression against it and refuses sovereign 'legitimate rights' to the Palestinians.

Actually this opposition to Palestinian aspirations is not restricted to the American approach. In fact, limiting the possibility of settling the Palestinian-Israeli antagonism to only one option, namely that an agreement be concluded ratifying the definite and irrevocable partition of the land of Palestine, boils down to endorsing this approach. Because if the Palestinians should not acquire the right of self-determination over the whole of their land, there is room for the argument that peace will be more readily attained by suppressing the Palestinian resistance rather than by dealing with it. Carried through to the end, this argument denies all sovereign rights to the Palestinians, in fact denies the very idea of an authentic partition of the land of Palestine. This logic makes of Israel, of its security and survival, the only fundamental consideration, and of the Palestinian problem nothing more than an obstacle to be neutralised.

Now is it true that peace is incompatible with meeting the Palestinians' basic demands? Is it inconceivable that peace can be achieved without jeopardising the Palestinians' right to self-determination over the whole of Palestine?

A clear distinction must be made between ultimate objectives and means of achieving them. The ultimate objectives of the Palestinians and the Israelis are incompatible; they cannot be reconciled. On the other hand, it is not inconceivable to replace mutually unacceptable, mutually detrimental modes of conflict by mutually tolerable ones, without affecting the basic incompatibility of the ultimate objectives. A current mistake is to believe that a settlement of the Palestinian-Israeli antagonism, and consequently peace in the Middle East, can only derive from an accommodation on the ultimate ends, not on the means of achieving them. But the first is impossible, the second is not.

Such an approach would certainly not be new. There have been precedents of this approach being used for settling the explosive issues since the onset of détente. A case in point is the US/USSR relationship where, although neither side has relinquished its goal of eliminating the other's ultimate objectives, both superpowers, under the threat of reciprocal nuclear extermination, strive to replace the arms race (a mutually detrimental mode of conflict) by economic competition (a mutually beneficial one). Each superpower believes that its economic system is better equipped to survive the other's. History will decide. Peace is possible not because ultimate objectives have been renounced, but because the means of achieving them have been modified.

Another case in point is the General Relations Treaty signed in 1972 between the Federal Republic of Germany and the German Democratic Republic. Though the Treaty normalises *de facto* relations between the two German states, neither state recognises *de jure* the other's existence. Since the Treaty was signed, a ruling of the Federal Constitutional Court in West Germany stipulated that both Germanies 'are part of a subsisting all-German State with one people' representing 'one nation' — a negation of the GDR — while the GDR upholds the opposite: that two German nations, one socialist, the other bourgeois, now confront each other, and there cannot be one German nation without the negation of the FGR as a bourgeois German nation.

What to make of these two illustrations?

The conclusion to be drawn is not to replace the spiral escalation or relentless confrontation with 'peaceful coexistence', as conditions for it are not met in the Palestinian-Israeli antagonism: the notion of parity introduced by the October war does not include the Palestinians, and while security borders are clearly established between East and West, between the socialist and capitalist worlds, this is not the case for confrontations between North and South, between movements of national liberation and neocolonialism. Israel still occupies not only the whole of Palestine, but also substantial chunks of Sinai and the Golan.

What should be realised is that the *de facto* establishment of two states in Palestine, one Israeli and the other Arab, is conceivable without mutual *de jure* recognition, and without either state having to renounce its ultimate objective of surviving the other or supplanting it. In fact, this concept implies neither a definite and irrevocable partition of the *land* of Palestine, nor a partition in the time dimension, meaning the immediate *substitution* of one state by the other. It is rather a synthesis of these two concepts inaugurating a process transcending both. This synthesis is the only means to ensure that the Palestinian people can recover their right to self-determination integrally without this contradicting the search for a settlement and the advent of peace.

We have already established that the absence of a Palestinian-Israeli agreement prevents even Egypt and Syria from regaining all their occupied territories. The crisis remains without solution. Peace is impossible. The step-by-step diplomacy has succeeded better in dissipating the disturbances brought about by the October war than in making this war a lever to generate a stable peace. It has only dealt with the peripheral problems. The process now is to be 'inverted' and we must go to the very core of the dispute. From now on, no real progress is possible without a clear understanding of the right

of the Palestinians to self-determination and the steps required
to implement it.

First, this right must be *asserted.* The cornerstone of the
Arab-Israeli conflict, the Palestinians, are nevertheless the only
party to the dispute who do not enjoy any sovereign right, who
are deprived of a state. This must be remedied. No remedy is
possible as long as no Palestinian territory whatsoever has been
recovered, a sovereign authority emanating from the PLO
established on it, and as long as this transfer of power is not
backed by the international community and endorsed by the
Security Council. This is not yet the Palestinian state. This
authority will not have established frontiers — in fact, no more
than Israel has. But in so far as a previous UN resolution,
resolution 181 adopted in 1947, had by recommending the
partition of Palestine been the act by which Israel was created,
it also legalised the right of the Palestinians to an equally
sovereign state. A disengagement on the Palestinian front,
under the auspices of the UN, is an indispensable step for the
materialisation of this state. This step would be decisively more
conducive than any other disengagement to an overall
settlement of the dispute.

Then Palestinian-Israeli negotiations must be initiated. The
issues on the agenda will be the configuration of the two states
in Palestine, their mutually agreed upon frontiers, and the rules
regulating their relationship. These negotiations will sooner or
later have to enter into the framework of the Geneva
Conference, with the active participation of all powers ready to
present guarantees.

Lastly, the PLO must be able to participate in these
negotiations without being requested to recognise Israel. There
is more than one precedent of this: the negotiations on Algeria
between France and the Provisional Revolutionary Government
and, more recently, the Vietnam negotiations.

Thus if a Palestinian-Israeli agreement will imply the
immediate renunciation of mutually unacceptable modes of
conflict, it must be in counterpart include a clause which
guarantees the possibility for the parties to continue working
towards their ultimate objectives, no matter how contradictory
they may be. If Israel is not required to renounce its Zionist
philosophy or the instrument by which it implements it, viz. the
Law of Return, then by the same token, Israel must not

interfere with the sovereign right of the Palestinian state to strive towards establishing a secular state in the whole of Palestine. In other words, if the agreement must commit each state not to violate the security and the sovereignty of the other, it must also stipulate the *de facto* character of the partition and include guarantees that the *de facto* arrangement will not acquire, *de facto* with time, the irrevocability of a *de jure* arrangement. No such clause exists either in Resolution 242 or in the previous UN Resolution on the partition of Palestine. It must be explicitly stated in the agreement.

One precondition of course is the immediate implementation of previous UN resolutions on the right of the Palestinian refugees to return or to receive compensation. As the Israeli state already includes an Arab minority whose ranks will swell after the return of a part of the refugees, it might be useful to retain a Jewish component under the sovereignty of the Arab Palestinian state, not only as a first rehearsal of the secular state, a test for its viability, but also a guarantee against second-class citizen treatment of Arabs in Israel.

But the real guarantee against an irrevocable partition of the land of Palestine is that the agreement must expressly stipulate that, under the auspices of the UN, referendums be held simultaneously and at appropriate intervals in the two states to decide whether both populations wish to remain separate or to replace partition by a unique state structure covering the whole of Palestinian territory. These referendums will continue to be held as long as the agreement under which they began in the first place has not been replaced by another. This condition is indispensable if the right of the Palestinian people to self-determination is not to be an empty slogan useful only in inducing them to renounce a part of their territory against their will. It is only the unequivocal affirmation and unconditional recognition of inalienable Palestinian rights that will credibly eliminate all doubts that the Palestinians will fail to fulfil their obligations. It is only this principled stand which can ensure that the legitimate rights of all concerned parties will be safeguarded and respected.

It must also be stressed that both states will not enjoy real sovereignty if the military balance tilts drastically in favour of one of them. There can be no question of demilitarising the Arab Palestinian state exclusively. Naturally the question of military parity is not limited to the Israeli and Palestinian states alone, but will extend to all states in the region involved in the conflict. Once an agreement is reached between Israel and the Palestinians on this basis, Israel can no longer use the argument by which it seeks to justify its refusal to withdraw from occupied territories outside Palestine. In return for total evacuation of these territories, the neighbouring Arab states could endorse *de jure* the *de facto* Israeli-Palestinian agreement. This is more consistent than granting Israel *de jure* recognition. But on the other hand it will mean that any violation of these agreements by any party will have to be condemned and opposed by all the other signatories.

Index